SIGNS
ON THE HORIZONS

"We shall show them Our Signs on the horizons
and in themselves,
till it is clear to them that it is the Truth.
Is it not enough that your Lord
is a Witness over everything?"

The Holy Qur'an*

For the people, in short, in joy and sorrow
He was an exemplar in the world, a sign.

Faridud-din 'Attar**

"The Saints are God's Signs
which He recites to His servants
by disclosing them one after another."

Abu'l Abbas Al Mursi***

* *Fussilat* 41:53.

** Speech of the Birds (*Mantiqu t-Tair*), translated by Peter Avery.
*** *Kitab Lata'if Al-Minan fi Manaqib Abu'l Abbas Al Mursi wa Shaykhihi Abu'l Hassan,,*
translated by Nancy Roberts.

SIGNS
ON THE HORIZONS

Meetings
with Men of Knowledge
and Illumination

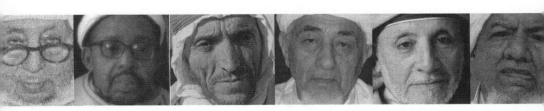

Michael Sugich

ISBN 978-0-9893640-1-0

Designed by Shems Friedlander

Cover Photo *View from Jebel Noor* by Peter Sanders

For my children

Kulthum, Muhsin, Abu Bakr, Sulafa, Ahmad and Habiba

And dedicated to the memory of Gai Eaton

CONTENTS

"Divine Wisdom Never Runs Dry."

Moulay Al-'Arabi Ad-Darqawi*

* Letters of a Sufi Master: The Shaykh Ad-Darqawi, translated by Titus Burkhardt..

INTRODUCTION

Memory for most of us is a compendium of our senses, vivid or muted images that resonate and remind us of time and age and achievement and loss. We experience our lives as a chain of events leading to each succeeding moment and we each live our personal history as its protagonist. In this continuum we find points of clarity and are touched by men and women who change us in some essential way. For most of humanity, it is our parents who shape us for better or for worse. For some, an individual – a teacher, a leader, an intellectual, an artist, a loving friend – someone stronger and more experienced than we are – someone who introduces us to another world. The impact these people have upon us is often inadvertent, sometimes misguided and occasionally inspired.

This is a book of memories, a commemoration of remarkable men who have defined my life, and I dare say, the lives of many others. While a few have been celebrated, most have passed through life in obscurity. Inwardly driven, they have had an alchemical impact on me for precisely the reason that they are unknown. They did not seek anything from the world; not recognition, position, wealth, influence, prestige or admiration. They were not ethereal or otherworldly, nor were they powerful in the sense most of us imagine saints and holy men to be. What characterized every one of these men was humility, kindness, sweetness of temper, patience, insight, and, most importantly, the remembrance of God at all times. By and large, they are men who have transcended the ordinary and achieved stations of spirituality and enlightenment we in the West only attribute to the Biblical fathers of ancient times or to myth. They are hidden treasures. At this writing, some are still alive but most have passed away. They are missed.

I've often wondered why I've had the great good fortune to have come into contact with these men. I am as worldly as the next

9

person and have done nothing to merit their attention. I'm not particularly adventurous. I'm not overly religious or contemplative. I am neither a scholar nor a saint. On reflection, I've come to the conclusion that my contact with these great men has been in direct proportion to my sense of distress, helplessness and need.

The 18th century Sufi Shaykh Ali Al-Jamal, said, "If people knew how many secrets and benefits are to be found in need, they would have no other need than to be in need." His successor, the sublime Shaykh Moulay Al 'Arabi Ad-Darqawi wrote, "Distress (*faqah*) is nothing but intensity of need." and "There is no doubt that, for men of God, their best moment is a moment of distress, for this is what fosters their growth." He refers to *Al-Hikam* of Ibn Ata'illah Al-Iskandari, saying, "The best of your moments is that in which you are aware of your distress and thrown back upon your own helplessness... it may be that in distress you will find benefits that you have been unable to find either in prayer or in fasting."*

Of course, we hate distress in our lives. We avoid it like the plague. I know I do. But it is in times of trouble, when we exhaust all our options and are forced to turn to God in extreme need, that we approach the essence of reality. One of the saints profiled in this volume, Moulay Abu'l Qasim, may God be well pleased with him, would say to us that there is nothing God loves more than His slave, helpless, weeping, with hands outstretched in supplication. He said this with tears of yearning in his eyes. Perhaps I have a greater sense of helplessness and need than many even though on the surface of things I appear to be strong and my life has been comfortable and relatively trouble free. When my sense of need has been strongest these men have appeared in my life, like divine instruments. When my feeling of helplessness has diminished and given way to a sense of empowerment and complacency or when I've been overcome by my passions and worldly concerns, these men have receded from

* Letters of a Sufi Master: The Shaykh Ad-Darqawi, translated by Titus Burkhardt.

my life and I miss them terribly.

When the Sufi Shaykh Abu'l Hassan Al-Shadhili was asked why he did not write books, he replied, "My companions are my books." Most of the men described in this volume are Sufis. Almost every one of them has been disciplined and guided – "written" – by a spiritual master. This volume is a personal celebration of this process.

Many of my contemporaries have had more profound and more prolonged contact than I with these and other great men of the Way, but have kept their own experiences to themselves. For many years I hesitated to commit these personal memories to writing partially because I considered the act of revealing these encounters to be close to hubris and partially because I was living in the Kingdom of Saudi Arabia where the practice of Sufism was banned by the religious authorities.

We have lost the meaning. We are living in an age that overwhelmingly revels in the world, alternating between euphoria and anxiety. We are oblivious to the subtle blessings and hidden realities that permeate existence. The men described on the following pages lived in the realm of meaning. They are signs on the horizons. Bless them all.

**"Surely being is meaning set up in images.
Those who grasp this are people of discernment."**

Shaykh Mohamed ibn Al-Habib*

* The Diwan: "Withdrawal into the Perception of the Essence".

ACKNOWLEDGEMENTS

I first conceived of the idea of writing about men of God (*Rijala 'llah*) that I have met over a quarter of a century ago when the photographer Peter Sanders and I discussed the idea of recording biographies of these men and others, in the tradition of the anecdotal hagiographies of saints that has existed in Islam since the beginning: *Khatam Al-Awliya* of Tirmidhi, *Tadhkirat Al-Awliya* of Attar, *Hiliyat Al-Awliya* of Abu Nu'aym and the *Ruh Al-Quds* and *Al-Durrat Al-Fakhirah* of Ibn Al-Arabi. We wanted to show in the most vivid way possible that men of profound spirituality are still with us. The project as originally conceived was more ambitious and would have required years of time and extensive travel to track down and interview hundreds of people who had known the great 20th century Sufis. However, we both had growing families and responsibilities that made the project highly impractical. For year after year we put this enterprise off, yet it was always at the back of both our minds. Both of us are passionate about the transcendent gifts these men have brought to our lives personally and to the world.

While the grand historical project we originally conceived has receded, we have each, separately, revived the idea in more personal forms. We are producing in parallel, two complementary volumes, both highly personal, from two different approaches. In a very real sense, this book would not have been written without the inspiration of Peter Sanders's four decade quest to capture the saints of Islam on film.

My initial motivation for writing this book was to share the experiences I have had with my children. I had never intended to publish the personal memories that form the content of this volume until my friend Shems Friedlander began putting together a wonderful journal on Sufism called "Zawiyyah". He was looking for articles to include in the first issue. I sent him a short piece on Moulay Abu'l Qasim, which he kindly included. The response to the article was surprisingly positive and made me realize that there was a thirst for this kind of shared experience. So this book found its form because of Shems Friedlander's creative initiative. More than this Shems has long been an inspiration for me as a gifted and courageously prolific author, film-maker, photographer, painter and publisher. Over the years we have collaborated on many and various projects and it was a foregone conclusion that he would design this volume.

I am also indebted to several of my close friends and companions on the Way. Shakir Massoud-Priest's vivid and generous recollections of the time he spent with some of the great Sufis described in this volume confirmed and enhanced my own memories. Shakir also contributed a unique photograph and gave me some invaluable editorial advice. The poet Daniel Abdul Hayy Moore, traded memories with me, bringing out some vivid descriptive detail. Abu'l Qasim and Aziza Spiker shared more memories with me of Morocco and our experiences on the Way and were my companions on the blessed journey to Moulay Hashem Balghiti. Aziza also did me the great service of reviewing and editing the text. Hamza Weinman was instrumental in connecting me to Moulay Hashem, and Azzadine Bettach has been a warm and wonderful support during my journeys to Morocco and a fount of wisdom and knowledge. And my thanks to my friend Abdallah Schleifer for his early encouragement.

In addition, I would like to pay tribute to the great translators and publishers who have made the traditional texts of *Tasawwuf* accessible in the English language through the years. When I was young the legendary Pakistani publisher Muhammad Ashraf came to call. When this thin, fastidious and venerable gentleman in a gray suit and red fez entered the room there was palpable excitement, for he had introduced generations of non-Arab seekers to the works of Al-Ghazali, Moulay Abdul Qadir Al-Jilani and other great Sufis for the first time. Several of my dear friends have taken the Ashraf legacy and raised it to new heights. Faarid and Aisha Gouverneur and Batul Salazar created the Islamic Texts Society, which pioneered a tradition of fine Sufi publishing that has been continued by the formidable, extraordinary Aisha (Gray Henry Blakemore) under the Fons Vitae imprimatur and Batul (Patricia) through her publishing house Archetype. The great British Sufi Arabist and professor T.J. Winter (Abdal Hakim Murad), has produced exquisite translations of Al-Ghazali's books of *Ihya Ulum Ad'din* and through his own publishing house, Quilliam Press, was the first to publish the writings of Habib Ahmad Mashhur Al-Haddad, translated by Dr. Mostafa Badawi, whose devotion to Al-Haddad is both unceasing and deeply moving. "The Letters of a Sufi Master, Moulay Al-Arabi Ad-Darqawi" has been my solace and my sustenance for 40 years and I am deeply beholden to its translator, the late Titus Burkhardt (Sidi Ibrahim). Abdul Rahman Fitzgerald has collaborated on many invaluable translations of classical Sufi texts, which have further enriched my understanding of the Way. Finally, I would like to pay tribute to Dr. Victor Danner, whom I had the privilege of taking on the Lesser Pilgrimage (*Umrah*) before he passed away, for his masterful translation of *Al-Hikam* of Ibn Ata'illah, may God have Mercy on him. I treasure the copy that he sent me. His widow, Dr. Mary Ann Koury-Danner, carried on her husband's work with an equally fine translation of Ibn Ata'illah's *Miftah al-Falah wa Misbah al-Arwah*. In many respects this book would have been impossible without the heroic efforts of these and others to bring the ancient knowledge to the English speaking world.

In 2009 I sent Gai Eaton, one of the most eloquent writers on Islam in our time, an early draft of the manuscript. He and I had performed *umrah* together in Makkah many years before and formed a bond of sorts, which was strengthened, for me at least, when my beloved mother was inspired to embrace Islam after reading "Islam and the Destiny of Man", his seminal interpretation of Islam for the West. Of late a trip to his home near Wimbledon had become a necessary feature of my layovers in London. On one of these visits I asked him what he thought of what I'd sent him. He was standing at his sideboard making tea for the two of us. He stopped, looked down and fell silent. After a pause, he said, "I am wrestling with my feelings." I said with some apprehension, thinking perhaps that he disliked what he'd read, "What do you mean?" He looked up and said, "Well I envy you." Surprised, I said, "Envy me? Why?" He said, "Because I led a sheltered life. I never had the courage to venture out and meet people like this. I wish I had." I said, "Well in my case it had nothing to do with courage and you are a great man and a great writer. You didn't need to." I learned that my friend was on his deathbed while I was driving. Overcome by grief, I pulled my car to the side of the road and wept. We have lost one of our greatest spokesmen and interpreters. In honor of his memory, I would like to dedicate this book to him, may God cover him with Mercy.

In conclusion, among these acknowledgements, I need to acknowledge my own extreme inadequacy. My association with the great souls I have remembered on these pages is a stroke of luck and a favor from God that I in no way deserve. I am under no illusions that their company has given me some special place in the scheme of things. I have fallen many times and continue to do so, but God is Oft-Returning and my hope is that He, may He be exalted, will forgive me and have mercy upon my soul.

**"All that I have done I reckon as but dust.
Whatsoever Thou hast seen of me not pleasing to Thy Presence,
do Thou draw the line of pardon through it.
And wash the dust of disobedience from me;
for I have myself washed away the dust
of the presumption that I have obeyed Thee."**

Abu Yazid Al-Bestami*

* Farid Al-Din Attar, Memorial of the Saints (*Tadhkirat Al-Auliya*) translated by A.J. Arberry.

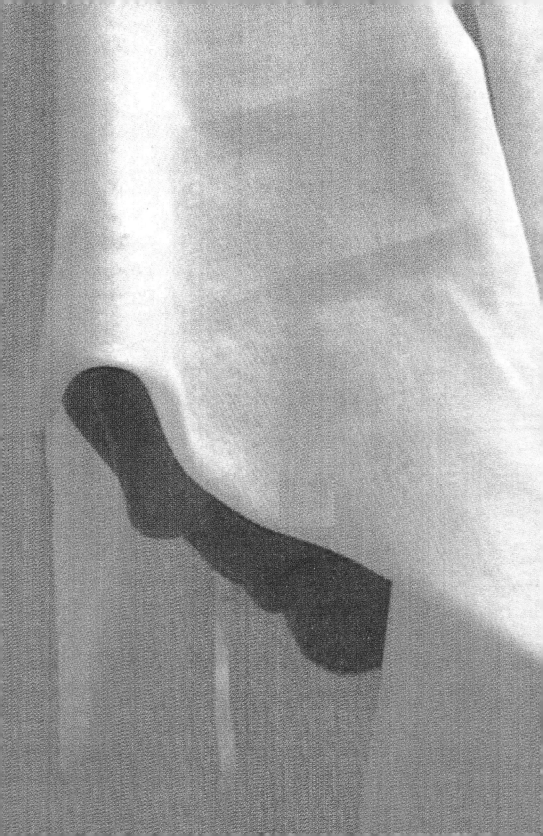

APPEARANCES

**"God's Friends are brides
and brides are not seen by criminals."**

Saying related by Ibn Ata'illah Al-Iskandari*

---

* The Subtle Blessings in the Saintly Lives of Abu Al-Abbas Al-Mursi and His Master Abu Al-Hasan, translated by Nancy Roberts.

THE HIDDEN

The Holy Mosque was an ocean of humanity during the days before the *Hajj*, the annual Pilgrimage to Makkah. As daylight faded I joined thousands of worshippers and pilgrims making the *tawaf*, the seven circuits around the Kaaba, calling out His Divine Names. As time approached for the sunset prayer, circular prayer lines formed around the House of God, rank by rank, closing around the vast *mataf*, the white marble floor surrounding the House all the way to the raised arcades designed by Sinan Pasha in the 16th century. The *mataf* was reduced, line-by-prayer-line, as individual worshippers peeled off from the shrinking *tawaf* to take their places in the encroaching ranks. I completed my seven circuits only moments before the call to prayer.

In a state of exaltation and hope, I knew that within this ocean there were deep seas of light and knowledge. I knew that among the hundreds of thousands of worshippers filling the Holy Mosque on every level there were the Close Friends of God, the *awliya'ullah*, God's saints. I also knew that I would never be able to recognize these men on my own. They were hidden by their humanity from ordinary souls like me. As I completed my *tawaf*, I asked God from the depths of my heart to show me one of His saints. Exhilarated by the light of the Holy Mosque, I prayed over and over again to meet one of His people. At that moment in time, intoxicated by the light that permeated the vast, roiling assembly, I yearned to meet at least one of the saints hidden in this tidal wave of pilgrims.

Caught in the slow-moving crush, each soul searching for a tiny space to join the prayer lines, I was pushed along a line of seated worshippers until the flow of the crowd abruptly stopped. Sitting before me in the prayer line was an old white-bearded man. I couldn't tell where he was from. I looked into his face. Tears were streaming down his cheeks. But they were not ordinary tears; he was weeping tears of blood. Blood was streaming from his eyes into his beard. There was no discernible emotion in his features, only an overwhelming serenity.

I leaned over and took his hand to kiss it. When he took my hand, a powerful electrical jolt passed through my arm straight to my heart. I kissed his forehead, looked into his weeping eyes again, and was swept away with the crowd.

**"O Lord of the Worlds,
I have foundered
Drowned in tears of blood,
my ship's driven ashore."**

Faridu-d Din 'Attar*

---

* The Speech of the Birds (*Mantiqu't-Tair*), translated by Peter Avery.

AN ORDINARY MAN

In the early 1970s the Qarawiyyin Mosque was still a gathering place for the Sufi Orders of Fes, and every evening after the sunset prayer *fuqara* (literally "the poor", members of Sufi brotherhoods) gathered in circles throughout the mosque to recite their evening litanies (*awrad*). My companions and I formed a circle and began reciting the *wird* (singular of *awrad*) of Shaykh Mohamed ibn Al-Habib. We were a small group, no more than about eight men. At the time I was young and easily agitated and my heart was in turmoil as we intoned the familiar liturgy. My eyes were lowered and closed as I wrestled with my turbulent heart and tried concentrating on the meaning of the collective voice from the circle of remembrance (*dhikru'llah* – invocation of God). I continued in this way until suddenly, without warning, my heart liquefied. I was immersed in a pool of light. The atmosphere became cool and diaphanous. My agitation vanished. I looked up to see if something had changed. A very ordinary man had joined our small circle. He was smiling. He was so ordinary looking that it was hard to believe that he had anything to do with my unexpected change of state. In fact, quite uncharitably, I saw him as an irritating intruder into our sacred circle. When we completed the *wird*, our guest went round the circle, kissed everyone's hand and departed.

His name, I came to learn, was Sidi Tami. Although ordinary on the outside, he had an extraordinary place in the spiritual hierarchy. He was the spiritual Guardian of Fes, chosen for this role by God, or this is what was accepted by the Sufi adepts. How this worked I never learned. Symbolically, concealed beneath his *djellaba*, he wore an immense set of prayer beads (*tasbih*) that extended all the way down to his knees. Few ever saw this. When he got to know us better, he once pulled the *tasbih* out. It was awesome. He then said casually with a wink and a smile and without a trace of self-importance, "Not too many people know this but I am a *wali'ullah* (literally, a Friend of God – a Saint)".

If anyone entered the labyrinthine ancient city of Fes from any gate with the intention of remembering God, they would "run into" Sidi Tami. There were times when three parties would come into different parts of the city unannounced from three different directions at the same time and they would all "by chance" just happen to meet him. He would then direct each party to different parts of the city to sit with spiritual adepts, join circles of remembrance or to visit the tombs of the saints.

On one such occasion, we entered from Bab Boujloud with no particular agenda and began walking into the bowels of the city. By this time we knew that we were bound to encounter Sidi Tami. We turned a corner and, sure enough, there he was. He took one of us by the hand and led the party down through the intricate cobbled walkways of Fes, deeper and deeper into the center of the city. He led us down a narrow side-street until we reached a low battered wooden door set within a scarred stone wall. Sidi Tami knocked on the door. When it opened the soaring voices of the Fes Singers broke through. We ducked under the small door as we passed through a magnificent medieval courtyard and into a large side room where a gathering of *dhikr* was already in progress. Hundreds of men were singing from the *diwans* of the saints, most from memory. The fabled Fes Singers were grouped at the center of a series of concentric circles, their accomplished voices rising above the assembly. The scene was dreamlike, electric, illuminated. The gathering was permeated with intoxicating perfumed smoke from the globular incense burners (*mabakhir*) that were circulated round and round the concentric circles. When the *mabkhara* reached each member of the assembly, he would pull the hood of his *djellaba* over his head and breathe in the exhilarating fumes. Some would lift up the hems of their *djellabas* and place the incense burner under their garments to capture the rich fragrance.

Other *fuqara* passed through the circles, waving rosewater

sprinklers over the devotees. Once the assembly reached a pitch of intensity, one of the organizers bypassed the ornamental etiquette of the nickel plated sprinkler, pulled the cork on a large bottle of rose water and waved the contents over the assembly, drenching the crowd in the heady perfume.

Glass after glass of sweet mint tea was passed through the crowd as we sang from the wisdom of the saints and invoked the remembrance of God until the *diwan* gave way to the *hadra* and the sacred dance began, lasting deep into the night. The evening ended with a recitation of the Holy Qur'an and a reflective discourse by one of the great scholars (*ulama*) of Fes. We reeled through the small door back up the winding streets through the intoxicating, luminous night; an evening courtesy of Sidi Tami.

Sometime later I was in Meknes at the *Moussem* of Shaykh Mohamed ibn Al-Habib. This was a week-long celebration revolving around the act of remembrance, morning, noon and night. After the noon prayer, *fuqara* tended to remain in the *zawiya* resting. Some slept, others chatted amongst themselves. Some drank tea. Some left to do errands or return to their families until the afternoon prayer. The day was hot and soporific. An unusual lethargy permeated the large *zawiya* hall.

Amongst the group was a strange but devoted Meknesi tinsmith who was known for his eccentric behavior and sudden, inappropriate outbursts in which he would leap up in the middle of a gathering and begin a solo *hadra*. He would always volunteer to wash the hands of the *fuqara*, carrying around a pitcher and an aluminum basin with a soap dish for hand-washing after a meal. In his case, once all the *fuqara* had washed their hands and mouths, he would lift the basin to his lips and drink down the used soapy water with relish, for the "*baraka*", or blessing. We always watched this odd spectacle with a mixture of amusement, revulsion and, I have to say, a kind of admiration at the mad devotion this *faqir* exhibited. There's a false assumption among the uninitiated and outsiders that the spiritual path is the exclusive domain of saintliness and sanity. This is not the case. The path is full of ordinary people. Some are sane, some are imbalanced, some advance, some stay behind. But the path provides a matrix for grace, and one person's inappropriate behavior can trigger another person's epiphany.

That sweltering afternoon, Si Fudul Al-Hawari Al-Sufi, the great Fesi scholar, began to give discourse to the gathering. He was an orator of shattering insight who could easily galvanize a crowd. In the midst of Si Fudul's sober oration in the quiet, languid afternoon, the tinsmith jumped up, eyes closed, and began his rhythmic solo *hadra*. On many occasions when this happened the *fuqara* ignored him or even interfered to stop him. On this occasion, Si Fudul waited for a moment and then he signaled the assembly to begin a formal *hadra*. Suddenly about fifty men formed a circle, all linking together by holding hands, and one of the most intense spiritual *hadras* I had ever participated in began. The dance was unbelievably powerful. Of the fifty people in the circle probably thirty were bona fide *awliya*. Every member was enrapt in the sacred dance, which eventually intensified into the exhalation *Hayy* (the Living), an accelerating collective breath. Outside the circle, *fuqara* with soaring mellifluous voices sang from the *Diwan* of Ibn Al-Habib.

The technique we were taught for concentration during the sacred dance was to visualize the Name of God - "*Allah*" in blazing white light against a blue horizon of sea and sky. The aim is to make the Mighty Name larger and larger until it fills one's vision, obliterates all thought and overtakes the heart. I was very inexperienced and my concentration was weak. I managed to keep the Name in my vision through the first part of the *hadra* but then my concentration wavered and the image of the Name vanished from my mind's eye. The moment the Name disappeared from my interior horizon, I felt the *faqir* on my right side squeeze my hand and pump my arm up and down to the rhythm of the *hadra* with great vigor, until the Name reappeared. I glanced over to my right. Sidi Tami, eyes closed, seemed completely absorbed in the back and forth rhythm of the sacred dance.

At first I thought that this might have been a fluke, but after losing sight of the Name several times and having Sidi Tami pump my arm until it returned, I knew it was no coincidence. It was as if he was inside me, seeing what I saw. This was no ordinary man.

**"Exalted be He Who makes His Saints known
only in order to make Himself known
and Who leads toward them those whom
He wishes to lead toward Himself."**

Ibn Ata'illah Al-Iskandari*

Al-Hikam translated by Victor Danner.

THE CARETAKER

He was, and, as of this writing is, the caretaker of the *Zawiya* (literally "corner" - the gathering place for a Sufi order) of Shaykh Mohamed ibn Al-Habib in Meknes. A pure Berber, he came to the Sufi Way through the most extraordinary circumstances and is living proof of the transformative power of spiritual practice. As a young man he was virtually without religion, working as a lumberjack in the Atlas Mountains. Throughout the history of Islam in Northwestern Africa the Berbers have had an ambivalent relationship with Islam, often reverting to their pre-Islamic pagan traditions or rejecting religion altogether only to be drawn back to Islam through the influence of one of the saints.

There is a story of a 19th century Sufi master who settled in the Atlas Mountains and began bringing the Berbers of the area back to Islam. Word of his achievement reached a scholar from the city who made his way to where the Sufi had settled to see for himself. When he entered the mountain village and approached the mosque, a mountain Berber galloped up on his horse, jumped off, brushed past the scholar, nearly knocking him over as he strode into the mosque with his boots on, walking across the carpeted floor toward the *qibla* – the direction of prayer. He stopped, said the *takbir* and performed his prayers. When the scholar met the Sufi he upbraided him. "Sidi, you are remiss. How can you let these people come into the mosque with their boots on?" The Sufi replied, "I got them into the mosque. It's your turn to teach them to take their boots off."

Sidi Ali lived a rugged, hard-drinking life in lumber camps in the Atlas Mountains without a thought for salvation until an accident that nearly took his life, changed his life. In Morocco logs from felled trees were loaded on flat-bed trucks and held in place with thick hemp ropes or chains. The bindings on one shipment Sidi Ali was loading broke and a massive log slid off the truck and crashed into his face, nearly killing him. He was taken to a hospital in a coma, where he hovered between life and death. He briefly emerged from the coma in darkness and silence; deaf, dumb, blind and paralyzed. In this abyss he swore that if he lived, the first thing he was going to do was to go to a mosque and embrace Islam. Then he relapsed into a coma.

When he finally regained consciousness he had the sight of one eye, the hearing in one ear, he could speak and had regained the use of his limbs. True to his oath, he dragged himself to a mosque near the hospital and re-entered Islam. He then returned to the hospital to recover from his catastrophic accident, which left him disfigured and disabled.

Throughout his convalescence he had a vivid recurrent dream. Every night in his sleep he would find himself sitting before a shaykh in a white cloak (*burnoose*). The shaykh methodically taught him a long recitation. When he awoke he found that he could remember portions of the recitation. This continued until he had memorized the entire litany, which lasted about 40 minutes. When he had completed memorizing the litany, the dream shaykh told him to come see him. He said, "My name is Mohamed".

When Sidi Ali finally recovered and was released from hospital, he limped to a local mosque to start a new life as a practicing Muslim. The first people he met there were members of a Sufi order. He told them about his dream and recited the litany he had learned by heart.

One of the *fuqara* recognized the litany. "This is the *Wird* of Mohamed ibn Al-Habib," he said.

"Where can I find him?" asked Sidi Ali.

"He resides in the city of Meknes."

Sidi Ali made his way north to Meknes and found the *zawiya* of Mohamed ibn Al-Habib. When he entered through the narrow passageway leading to the large mosque area where the *fuqara* gathered, he was met by the guardian of the *zawiya*, Sidi l'Ayyashi, a stern, imposing figure and meticulous disciple of the Shaykh. Sidi Ali knew nothing of Islam, much less Sufi protocol. He marched into the *zawiya* and simply asked where Mohamed was. Sidi l'Ayyashi said, "Who?"

"Mohamed, Mohamed," Sidi Ali shrugged. "He told me to come to him."

"Do you mean Our Master Shaykh Mohamed ibn Al-Habib?"

"I don't know. Yes, I guess so."

Sidi l'Ayyashi looked skeptically at this squinting, funny-looking little man before him. He told him to wait there and ascended the stairs to the Shaykh's quarters to tell him of the curious visitor. Shaykh Mohamed ibn Al-Habib instructed the guardian to bring the visitor up to his apartment.

When Sidi l'Ayyashi returned to the *zawiya* mosque he asked Sidi Ali whether he had *wudhu*, that is, whether he was in a state of ritual ablution, as it was the custom of the Sufis to be in a state of ritual purity when in the presence of a spiritual master.

"What's *wudhu*?" Sidi Ali asked.

Sidi l'Ayyashi shook his head in disbelief and patiently showed the young half-blind Berber how to perform the ritual ablution. Then he escorted him upstairs to the Shaykh's living quarters. When Sidi Ali entered the room he saw the man who had appeared to him every night in his dreams. And Shaykh Mohamed ibn Al-Habib said, "We've been waiting for you."

I first met Sidi Ali in 1973 and heard this story from his lips. He was living in the *zawiya*, helping Sidi l'Ayyashi to take care of the premises. When Sidi l'Ayyashi passed away during the 1980s, Sidi Ali became the guardian of the *zawiya*. Completely illiterate, he has memorized large parts of the Qur'an and the entirety of the *Diwan* of Mohamed ibn Al Habib in addition to

27

many Prophetic traditions, wisdom sayings and odes from the Sufis. He's now totally blind and mostly deaf. He carries a card from the Moroccan government certifying that he is officially indigent (*miskeen*) that entitles him to beg, which he sometimes does when the guests in the *zawiya* need to be fed and there is no money. He flashes this card with a mischievous laugh. When I saw him in 1981, he told me proudly and with a chuckle, as if he had achieved the impossible, "You know, I got married."

I traveled with Sidi Ali to the desert in 1981 to visit one of the greatest living saints in Morocco, Sidi Mohamed Bil Kurshi. There were three of us plus Sidi Ali, who knew the road to Touroug, the *ksar* where the great Sufi lived, which lay in the Sahara beyond the Atlas. We drove through the afternoon and stayed overnight in a desert village. It was winter and bitterly cold, so cold in fact that many local people do not perform their ritual ablutions (*wudhu*) with water during winter. If they do their hands and feet become deeply cracked and damaged. They perform waterless ablution, or *tayyamum*, with dust or stone instead. But as I was only passing through I insisted upon performing *wudhu* with well water. They looked at me as if they thought I was mad, but drew water from the well for me at dawn. I began to perform my ritual ablution. When the icy well water touched my skin I felt as if I was being stabbed with knives. It was excruciatingly painful. After breakfast we set off toward Touroug.

We drove through the day further and further into the desert. At midday Sidi Ali insisted that we stop for the noon prayer but I insisted that we press on to reach Touroug early, before nightfall. We were, after all, in a state of travel and could join our prayers. Sidi Ali shook his head and said quietly. "We really should stop for the prayer." We ignored him and drove on, closer and closer to Touroug. The time for the afternoon prayer arrived and Sidi Ali reminded us that we should stop for both prayers. We were so close to Touroug that I said we would do our prayers once we arrived. Again, Sidi Ali shook his head and said quietly, "We really should stop for the prayers." Again, we ignored him. We drove on and on and became hopelessly lost. The sun was getting lower on the horizon. Sidi Ali said quietly, "I'm telling you we should stop for the prayer." Finally, I relented. We stopped and prayed both prayers together. When we got back on the road, we instantly found the track leading to Touroug. Sidi Ali said, by way of quiet admonition, "I told you we needed to stop for the prayers."

About 15 years later one of my close friends visited Sidi Ali in the *zawiya* in Meknes. They were sitting together and, in passing, Sidi Ali mentioned that the week before his sight had gone completely. He sighed in resignation. "I was able to see shadows before. Now there is nothing."

Here is a man who by all conventions should have been a denizen of the lower depths of society: ignored, illiterate, disfigured, limping, penniless, blind and deaf. Almost anyone in his place would be bitter, miserable and without hope. Yet here is a man whose constant invocation, dedication to service and association with living saints transformed him into an inestimable gift, a man of knowledge, wisdom, certainty, kindness, lightness of heart and peace.

He is, for me, the personification of the words of Shaykh Moulay Al-'Arabi Ad-Darqawi: "Certainly all things are hidden in their opposites – gain in loss and gift in refusal, honor in humiliation, wealth in poverty, strength in weakness, abundance in restriction, rising up in falling down, life in death, victory in defeat, power in powerlessness …"

"When He opens up your understanding of deprivation, deprivation becomes the same as giving."

Ibn Ata'illah Al Iskandari*

* *Al-Hikam*, translated by Victor Danner.

AN OVERFLOW OF ECSTASY

Outwardly he was unremarkable, a clean-shaven, bespectacled, bourgeois gentleman, fastidious in an immaculate *djellaba* and red fez. He owned a small shop in Casablanca that, if I remember correctly, sold buttons or fabric or ribbon. He was a family man. His children took piano lessons. His life was, on the surface of things, ordinary. The surface of things is, of course, deceptive.

I first met him in a passageway leading to the main *zawiya* hall in Meknes. I was always very hard on myself, and the first year I visited the Sufis of Morocco I was in a perpetual state of shock. I had spent most of my youth in the theater and was characteristically narcissistic. Suddenly I was thrown into the company of men who had virtually no self-regard, but who spent every waking moment remembering God. They couldn't have been less interested in my past, personality or my emotions. They were only interested in remembering God.

Of course I went along with all this on the outside but inwardly my ego was screaming, "What about ME?!!" I had just completed my ritual ablutions and joined a crowd of *fuqara* entering the *zawiya*. My heart was constricted and it must have shown on my face. As he walked past me he looked me in the eye, smiled sweetly and flipped his hand, palm up, as if to say, "Lighten up." He pointed to the sky and said, "Don't worry, remember God." I remember thinking petulantly, "That's all very well for you to say, but you are not a self-involved, neurotic wreck like I am." Silently, I wished I could be untroubled like this infuriatingly normal fellow appeared to be.

A few days later we were told that a very great saint was coming to visit. We gathered together in anticipation. The gentleman in the passageway arrived. His appearance was less than impressive. He had none of the romantic Arabian Nights mystique about him that some of the other Sufi saints we met possessed. He looked exactly like the shopkeeper that he was. The only thing I noticed that set him apart was that he seemed to be in a constant state of remembrance, repeating invocations and supplications (*du'aa*) under his breath from the moment he entered to the moment he left.

He sat before us, eyes lowered. He sat for what seemed like a long time, lips moving in silent supplication. The atmosphere became charged, transcendent. He exhaled the Name of God slowly. Then, without introduction, he began to speak.

His talk was aphoristic and seemingly random, almost like a stream of consciousness. He would say something, wait in silence and then he would say something else entirely unrelated. Yet, I noticed that each time he spoke his words seemed to have a profound impact on a single member of the audience. Whenever he said something someone would quietly exclaim, *"Allah!"* or *"Masha'Allah!"* ("So God wills"), as if he was speaking directly to that person, as if his words struck the heart. One by one, his speech hit each member of the audience. He was speaking heart to heart to heart. I can't remember what he said that struck me personally but I remember his words hit me hard.

What I do remember vividly – and this memory will never leave me as long as I live – was the awesome transformation we witnessed. It was like watching an accident of nature; the eruption of a volcano, the formation of a tsunami, the approach of a cyclone.

Gradually, as he spoke of God, he began to tremble. His eyes filled with tears. He looked toward his listeners but he saw something else. His eyes widened. He began to weep uncontrollably. He began shaking. Overwhelmed, his deep sighs became intense heaving. He swayed in awe. He looked into the distance, crying out the name of God. The atmosphere brimmed with an overflow of ecstasy.

We watched in stunned silence as this unassuming, quiet shopkeeper, became a raging, crazed, drunken lover: Majnun crying out for Layla. He left the gathering in a state of utter devastation, sobbing, supplicating, calling out the Names of God, and leaning on one of our companions for support. He had swamped us with passion. He had shown us a glimpse of the overwhelming power of Divine Love.

"Oh Distracter of Lovers, arise and openly proclaim! Fill us to the brim and refresh us with the Name of the Beloved."

Shaykh Abu Madyan Shu'ayb*

* *Qasida in Nun* in The Way of Abu Madyan, translated by Vincent Cornell.

A BLACK ANT
ON A BLACK STONE

One walked past them or around them with barely a glance. They were a background feature, local color – the dregs of society, forgotten, anonymous – these beggars who gathered outside the mosques of the Old City of Meknes between the prayers and at the edge of marketplaces. They were all registered as officially indigent (*miskeen*) and thus legally permitted to take alms. Even so, the authorities would periodically round them up and clap them in jail to clear the streets. Most suffered from a severe infirmity. Among them was a blind man who sat patiently in his position every day and waited for his provision.

He had been blind from childhood, the victim of trachoma, a disease transmitted by flies, often to young children. He would pass his days performing invocations (*dhikru'llah*) and occasionally chat with his fellow beggars. He never asked passersby for alms. He simply sat outside the mosque patiently. He was always pleasant, always smiling. At the end of the day, he would wrap his coins in a white handkerchief, pull himself up by his cane and make his way back through the winding cobbled streets of the Old Town to the *zawiya* where he lived.

Si Khlefa shared a room off the public area with other *fuqara*. He had few possessions. He shaved his head, so he didn't need a comb. He was blind, so he didn't need a mirror. He had an *arak* stick to clean his teeth and a bar of soap to wash with, and he had a small purse to keep the coins he collected. He would put each coin in his mouth to determine its denomination. He had only one change of clothes, which he kept scrupulously clean. He may have had an extra pair of socks and an extra handkerchief. I don't know. Whatever he did possess he meticulously stored in his bedroll, which he put away in a cupboard every day. He left no trace. I once saw him washing his grey *djellaba* and turban by hand. He wore a long undershirt and had to remain in his underclothes until his *djellaba* dried in the sunlight.

One day he failed to return to the *zawiya* and went missing for many days. The *fuqara* were very worried but no one could find him. Then, without warning, he returned to the *zawiya* in a much weakened state. The police had made one of their periodic sweeps, threw Si Khlefa in jail and forgot about him. He did not eat anything for one week.

His sense of good humor never flagged. Blind eyes closed, he smiled constantly, laughed easily. He was satisfied with his place in the world. His face had a luminous moon-like quality. He never ceased invoking God.

He is a hidden treasure, the incarnation of the Sufi aspiration to "be like a black ant on a black stone at midnight".

"If I deprive My servant of his two eyes in this lower world, I shall give him in compensation nothing less than Paradise."

Hadith Qudsi*

* *Mishkat al-Anwar* of Ibn 'Arabi translated Stephen Hirtenstein and Martin Notcutt.

THE MU'ADHIN OF SEFROU

I would never have noticed Hajj Mohamed Al-Khidra'a had not one of my companions pointed him out to me in a large gathering of Sufis in Meknes in 1975. He did not have an imposing appearance. He was an elderly man in his 70s or 80s, white bearded, with a high forehead and wearing the dark green turban of the Darqawa, lost in the crowd, head bowed, reciting Sufi odes (*qasa'id*). We somehow expect men of spiritual attainment to have an obvious beatific presence. This is sometimes the case, but more often than not the saints are wrapped in anonymity.

He had been the *mu'adhin* – the one who delivers the call to prayer - of Sefrou, a small village outside Fes. He was, I was told, a very great saint. For many years he had lived in a state of extreme dread (*khawf*) of God. This is an exalted and terrible spiritual condition on the Way in which the Sufi is overwhelmed with fear and paralyzed by a direct experience of God's Majesty (*Jalal*). According to Moulay Abdul Qadir Al-Jilani, in *Futuh Al-Ghaib*:

"*Al-Jalal* produces a disquieting fear and creates disturbing apprehension and overpowers the heart in such an awful manner and its symptoms become visible on the physical body."*

According to *fuqara* who knew him at the time, Hajj Mohamed lived for years in a state of paralysis and terror, rarely speaking and weeping copiously. He constantly trembled with fear and was repeatedly struck by what the Sufis call Lightning (*Barq*), which is a spiritual event where a powerful electric-like wave shoots from the base of the spine through the neck like a light-

---

* *Futuh Al Ghaib*, translated by M. Aftab-ud-din Ahmad

ning bolt. When this happens, the *faqir* should cry out the Name of God ("*Allah!*") and then lower the eyes and say a blessing on the Prophet Mohamed, peace be upon him. The experience can be shattering and hits certain people on the path from time to time. In Hajj Mohamed's case lightning struck him over and over again for years. The impact is hard to imagine.

By the time I met him he had passed through this station transformed, and was now basking in the Beauty (*Jamal*) and Mercy (*Rahma*) of God. His whole manner was effusive, light and overflowing. He was childlike, innocent and unreservedly sweet. Moulay Abdul Qadir Al-Jilani described this condition in *Futuh Al-Ghaib* as the Divine "reflection on the heart of man producing light, joy, elegance and sweet words and loving conversation and glad tidings with regard to great gifts and high position and closeness to Himself..."**

A few days later Hajj Mohamed came to us and spoke. He could barely contain himself. He was like a shimmering river. It was as if he were reporting excitedly from the vantage point of Paradise. His entire talk consisted of ways to get to Heaven, what happens there and the overwhelming Mercy of God. Everything seemed to well up within him. It all seemed so accessible, so close. He was utterly convincing, simple and sane. I had been similarly impressed by the quiet assurances of the illuminated saint Moulay Abu'l Qasim*** but whereas Moulay Abu'l Qasim spoke infrequently and with deep ecstatic gravitas, Hajj Mohamed inundated us with glad tidings. He spoke for hours. I remember he admonished us all always to complete our supplications (*du'aa*) to God with the invocation, *Ya Dha l'Jalali wa l'Ikram* ("Oh Lord of Majesty and Gifts"). This, he said, was a seal that would ensure our prayers would be answered. He also told us, "When things are going well have fear (*khawf*) of God and when things are going badly have hope (*raja*) in God."

When he finished, we all left together to attend a *laylat al-fuqara* (literally, "night of the poor" - a night of invocation). We walked

** Ibid.
*** See First Light, page 85.

as a group from the courtyard house we were renting in the old city to the home of one of the wealthy *fuqara* who had invited us for the evening. Hajj Mohamed's talk had left me completely exhilarated and as we walked I fell in to step with him. In his discourse he had said that with every step one took with the *tahlil* (*la ilaha illa 'llah* – no god but Allah) on one's tongue, one built a castle in Paradise. As we walked silently side-by-side, both of us invoking the *tahlil*, I was filled with the sensation that this was actually happening. Before we parted company that evening Hajj Mohamed invited us to come and visit him in Tangiers.

After this sublime evening I led a group of *fuqara* to the Middle Atlas. On the way back I fell asleep during a bus ride. On awakening in Khenifra, I found that my wallet with all my money and passport had been stolen. I was originally supposed to travel to Algeria but found myself stuck in Morocco without passport and penniless. I borrowed a little money and made my way on a wooden train from Meknes to Tangier where the U.S. Consulate General was, to try and get a replacement passport and wire England for enough money to get back to London. This was not the first time in my life I was completely alone, reduced to poverty and almost absolutely helpless, but it was the first time this had happened to me in a foreign country. I had the equivalent of about $5.00 after my train fare, passport expenses and the cost of a telegram.

I made my way to the Siddiqui *Zawiya* in the ancient part of Tangiers and, in the time-honored tradition of the Sufis, requested lodging. After explaining my circumstances, the caretaker of the *zawiya*, showed me to a windowless cupboard behind the *qibla* wall of the mosque, with a small bed. I gratefully accepted.

The first day I was at the *zawiya* I joined the weekly *laylat al-fuqara*. I sat in the back of the gathering in a state of extreme helplessness. As *qasa'id* from a *diwan* were sung by the large assembly I began to remember Hajj Mohamed for no particular reason. His beautiful old face loomed up in my mind's eye and filled my heart. An overwhelming desire to see him welled up within me. I knew he lived in Tangier but had no idea how to find him. I longed to see him and began to weep, his face etched in my memory, the sound of remembrance surrounding me.

I put my face in my hands and wept for a very long time. At the conclusion of the first phase of the invocation the gathering began to recite the *La ilaha illa 'llah* over and over again in a wonderful lilting melody I had never heard before. My weeping subsided. I looked up and across the circle I saw Hajj Mohamed. It seemed as if he didn't notice me but when the assembly stood to perform the *hadra* Hajj Mohamed purposefully moved around the circle beside me and took my hand. We performed the *hadra* hand in hand. At the end of the dance, he turned to me, kissed my hand in greeting and departed. In a state of high excitement, I rushed to the caretaker of the *zawiya* and pointed out Hajj Mohamed's departing figure. I asked him if he knew him. He said, "No, I've never seen him before. He never comes here."

After accepting lodging at the Siddiqui *Zawiya* I privately vowed to myself not to ask anyone for anything more. I used most of the money I had left to purchase oranges and *svinges*, Moroccan style doughnuts. I subsisted on this fare for 3 days. On the third day, I began to become weak and ill. The greasy *svinges* and the acidity of the oranges gave me severe stomach pains. After the noon prayer on the third day, I raised my hands in supplication and asked silently, "O God, I'm getting sick and this will put my hosts to more trouble. Please, please feed me so that I can keep up my strength."

The moment I finished my supplication, a young man about my age sitting beside me turned and struck up a conversation with me. It was the usual sort of encounter one had in mosques. I was accustomed to conversations with young Muslims from the Arab world fascinated with the West and Westerners, amazed that an American or European would want to become a Muslim and come to their countries, when most of them dreamed of the exotic, wealthy West. It was a typical exchange, mostly about me being from America. I mentioned that I was staying in the *zawi-*

ya but that was all. Almost as an afterthought, he asked me if I'd had lunch. Keeping in mind my vow, I lied and told him that I'd already eaten but he suddenly insisted that I come upstairs with him to eat. I couldn't believe it. It was the answer to my prayers. From that moment on, without ever asking, I was fed morning, noon and night for three weeks and by the end of this period I was not so much being fed as feasted as a guest of eminent Moroccan scholars. I never had to ask for anything.

The young man who first invited me was named Mustafa. He was from Tetouan and had spent years working in factories in Spain because he couldn't find work as an Imam, which is what he had been trained for. He had been the Imam of a mosque in Tetouan and was *hafiz* of Qur'an (one who has memorized the entire Qur'an). He recited Qur'an with a stunning, angelic voice. He lived upstairs in the Siddiqui *Zawiya* with his uncle, who had a position in the Siddiqui Sufi Order, and a number of other young *huffaz* (plural of *hafiz*) in similar circumstances. Mustafa took me under his wing, mainly I think because he was fascinated by America and because we both spoke broken Spanish and could communicate (I didn't know a word of Arabic at the time).

Two days later I was walking in the *Nouvelle Ville* (New Town) with Mustafa. He told me about his frustrations and desire to get married; how girls were not interested in men who knew Qur'an, but wanted to marry men who were worldly and had money. As we climbed up the steep hill from the Old Town to the *Nouvelle Ville* I found myself thinking about Hajj Mohamed. I thought to myself, "I hope we meet him and I hope he invites me to lunch." The moment this thought came to mind – I'm not exaggerating – we turned a corner and standing before us was Hajj Mohamed. He beamed, kissed our hands and said, "*Salamskum!* Would you like to come to lunch with me?" I was overjoyed. Hajj Mohamed asked us to come the next day and showed us where his house was in the New Town. He took us on a tour of his home, which was an apartment in a modern block of flats. He was particularly pleased with his European-style bathroom (*hammam faranji*), which he showed us with almost childlike pride. We then promised to return the following day and took our leave.

I asked Mustafa to join me for lunch the next day. I needed him to translate for me. He was not enthusiastic. He said he was not sure if he could. I pleaded with him. In my excitement and to convince him to come with me I said, "He is a great saint (*wali'ullah*)."

At this, Mustafa stopped suddenly and scolded me, "You mustn't say that! If he's a *wali*, I'm a *wali*, you're a *wali*! A *wali'ullah* is someone very rare and special. He's a sweet old man, but you mustn't call him a *wali'ullah*. This is something very serious."

I replied defensively, "I didn't make this up. I've been told by people of authority that he's one of the *awliya*."

Mustafa wasn't convinced. "I don't think so," he said.

I said, "Okay but please come with me tomorrow." He said, "I'll see. I'm not sure."

The next day I managed to drag Mustafa out of the *zawiya* up the hill to the *Nouvelle Ville* for our luncheon engagement. We came to the flat at the appointed time. Hajj Mohamed's wife answered the door and said that he had gone out and would be back soon. She asked us to come back in half an hour.

We retired to a nearby park overlooking Tangier Harbor to wait. I could see Mustafa was becoming impatient and began to worry that he'd abandon me. In the park he ran into a friend of his. I waited for half an hour, looking out over Tangier and the harbor. Mustafa was engaged in conversation with his friend and showed no interest in returning to Hajj Mohamed's. I waited as long as I could and then said to Mustafa that I was going on ahead back to Hajj Mohamed's house. "Please join me when you're done here," I pleaded. Mustafa said that he might but I wasn't optimistic.

I made my way back to the block of flats and ascended the stairs to Hajj Mohamed's flat. He opened the door when I knocked, beaming, greeting me with "*Salamskum!*" I greeted him back and gave him a pot of honey I had purchased with the little money I had left. He was thrilled and thanked me profusely. His happiness made my heart sing. I felt that I had done the right thing. He led me to a sitting room off the entrance and sat me on a couch beside him. There were two cups of sweet milky coffee on the coffee table in front of him. I assumed one was for him and one was for me. He moved both in front of me and smiled. We smiled at each other but couldn't communicate. He shrugged. I shrugged and sipped my coffee. I was incredibly frustrated, but could do nothing. Hajj Mohamed excused himself and went into another room. He sat down when he returned and we looked at each other helplessly. I could tell he wanted to say things to me, but it was no use. I prayed that Mustafa would turn up.

Finally, after about 20 minutes the doorbell rang. Mustafa had arrived after all. Hajj Mohamed greeted him with his buoyant "*Salamskum!*" kissed his hand and led him to the couch, sitting between the two of us. He then turned to Mustafa with a twinkling eye and said something to him in Arabic, which made Mustafa's jaw drop. Mustafa looked over at me, stunned. I asked eagerly, "What did he just say?" Mustafa said in shock, "He said, 'I just wanted to let you know that I really am a *wali'ullah*.'" I almost burst out laughing.

The three of us had an incredible lunch. Hajj Mohamed was irrepressible. He told us that when he was in Makkah at the Ka'aba an angel appeared to him and told him that the Blast of Israfil would take place in 22 years. According to Sufi scholars, the trumpet blast of Israfil signifies the destruction of the world and the end of time. He added, "So be careful of your religion". This was in 1975, which would have meant, if we were to take Hajj Mohamed literally, that the world would end in 1997. Of course, we are still here. This illustrates something else that is often misunderstood about the *awliya'ullah*. Many outsiders and the uninitiated assume that sainthood (*wilayat*) is equated with infallibility. According to Shaykh Saleh Al-Ja'fari, the difference between a Prophet and a saint is that Prophets are not allowed to make mistakes – they are, he said, "disciplined by

41

God" - but *awliya'ullah* can and do make mistakes. God disciplines the Prophets and Messengers. God's saints are illuminated and possessed of deep spiritual knowledge but they are not infallible. Shaykh Abdul Qadir 'Isa reinforces this point, saying that the disciple should "not believe his Shaykh to be infallible. Even if the Shaykh is in the best of spiritual conditions, he is still not infallible."**** The most important part of Hajj Mohamed's message was the admonition, "Be careful of your religion."

He was also adamant that when we sat in circles of *dhikr* we should not interlock our fingers in our laps, but put one palm in another. He said that the Devil (*Shaytan*) sits with interlocking fingers.

Everything Hajj Mohamed said was linked to practical instruction, basically on how to get to heaven. It was hard to believe that this old man had been shaking with fear less than two years before. He was effusive, joyful, serene and overflowing with good news.

The three of us recited from the Diwan of Mohamed ibn Al-Habib and performed a *hadra*. Hajj Mohamed's wife joined us, standing apart from the three of us. She seemed a strange old woman. Mustafa recited from the Qur'an. His voice was ravishing. Hajj Mohamed wept. His wife also wept intensely, almost hysterically.

When his wife left the room, Hajj Mohamed shook his head and said sadly, "She's insane. I cured her once but she has relapsed. I am trying to cure her again, God willing." He obviously loved her deeply. She was very sweet but very disturbed.

This exchange was a poignant reminder of the nature of the *awliya*. They are men and women, with human frailties and facing the same troubles and tragedies we all face. Some are wealthy, most are not. Some have wonderful, happy families; some have troubled children or demented wives. Sainthood does not guarantee a trouble-free existence in this life. It guarantees a trouble-free existence in the next life and wisdom to bear the

**** From The Realities of Sufism, translated by Suraqah Abdul Aziz

42

trials of being alive.

I wanted to keep company with Hajj Mohamed as much as possible but couldn't expect Mustafa to accompany me every time I visited him, so I took to paying him visits during the day. We didn't talk but sat silently together. I loved his wordless presence. I was so gratified by his response to my gift of honey that I purchased a small bag of sugar with the last of my meager funds to bring with me on my second visit. I was worried about money but bought the gift as much to get the same response from him as to not come empty-handed. In other words, my gift was not spontaneous, from the heart, as my honey pot had been but, rather, something I saw as obligatory.

When Hajj Mohamed answered the door, I gave him the sugar. He frowned and said sharply, "Don't do that again!" It was an admonition to act from the heart, not from the head.

When we sat together Hajj Mohamed would often suddenly get up. He would tell me to wait and he would leave the house and return half an hour or forty minutes later. I came to understand that he was called away through some kind of inspiration, in the way that he had crossed my path to treat my ailing heart. He was an instrument of destiny, acting in concealment, touching ordinary lives, anonymously, without fanfare.

This station is described by Shaykh Mohamed ibn Al-Habib in his *Diwan*:

"When they make an action, there is no question but that they are just like instruments moved by Divine Decrees."

During my long layover I was becoming a part of the small community of Sufis in Tangier. I was invited to the homes of scholars and other Sufis. I would perform the Siddiqui *wird* in darkness after the dawn prayer with two or three devoted *fuqara*. I would eat lunch daily with a very aged imam who ate in incredibly slow motion. To be courteous, I tried to keep his pace but found it almost impossible. I had submitted my application for a new passport to the US consulate but they needed to send it to the embassy in Rabat for approval. Weeks passed. I would check every few days. Finally, the Consul informed me that the passport would be ready. I was to pick it up at 7 a.m. in the morning. I had wired to my work in London for an advance on my salary and had already received funds to get me back to London. I booked passage on a boat to Algeciras, which was to leave at 8:30 a.m. in the morning.

I walked up the hill from the Siddiqi *Zawiya* to the U.S. Consulate to receive my new passport. All the way up the hill and all the way down I kept debating whether I should pay a quick visit to say farewell to Hajj Mohamed. I could have made a side trip on the way back to the Old City but it was about 7:30 a.m. and I wasn't sure whether Hajj Mohamed stayed awake after the dawn prayers or, as many people did, returned to sleep. In any case, it felt awkward to simply knock on the door to say goodbye – a little like my not very well received obligatory gift of sugar.

With a pang of regret I carried on down the hill, bag and passport in hand, into the *Socco Checo*, the central square in the old town. The square was completely deserted, not a soul to be seen. All the shops were still closed. A café on the square with an outdoor terrace was just opening. I walked in to the bar and ordered a coffee. When I turned around to walk back out to sit on the terrace, perfectly framed by the door, standing alone across the square, was Hajj Mohamed. It was like a scene in a movie. It took my breath away.

I put my bag down by the table and walked straight toward him. We were alone in the *Socco Checo*. As I approached him he seemed to be preoccupied with something in a small shoulder purse. I greeted him. He looked up and seemed surprised to see me, as if this was pure coincidence.

I told him I was leaving. He prayed for me and said to come back to see him sometime. I knew we would never meet again. He then turned and made his way back up the hill toward the *Nouvelle Ville*. I turned back to the café and my coffee and then made my way toward the dock to take the boat to Algeciras.

It was the last time I ever saw this great soul. I will never forget him. May God be well pleased with him.

"It is more difficult to recognize the friend of God than it is to recognize God Himself. After all, God is recognized by virtue of His perfection and beauty. By contrast, how long will it take you to come to know another creature like yourself, who eats as you eat and drinks as you drink?"

Abu'l Abbas Al-Mursi*

* The Subtle Blessings in the Saintly Lives of Abu Al-Abbas Al-Mursi and His Master Abu Al-Hasan, translated by Nancy Roberts.

ROCK CANDY

During the early 1970s we encountered the last vestiges of traditional Sufism in Morocco, alive with the gatherings of saints and ecstatics, men of transcendent knowledge and blazing illumination. The gross materialism that has long since overwhelmed societies across the Muslim world was only beginning its inevitable corrosive subversion of tradition and spirituality. Televisions and refrigerators were novelties only the rich could afford. Advertising had not yet reached the interiors. Traditional bazaars were the only shopping centers. The mosques were filled with worshippers and the litanies of the people of the Path were still a feature of Muslim life.

As novices we were naturally captivated by the great Sufi saints, some of whom are described on these pages. In the background were *fuqara* who had utterly devoted themselves to service (*khidma*) and remembrance of God; serving tea and food, shopping, sweeping up, cleaning the *zawiya*, collecting money to pay bills, making repairs to the building, all because of their devotion to their Shaykh and for a reward in the Afterlife. Unrecognized, taken for granted, these men formed the backbone of the Sufi orders and kept the Path alive.

One of the first people I met in Morocco was the guardian of the *Zawiya* of Mohamed ibn Al-Habib in Meknes. His name was Sidi l'Ayyashi, which meant that he hailed from the village of Ayyash. He had been a builder and had, many decades before, been one of the stone-masons who had built the *zawiya*. In his later years he lived in and watched over the *zawiya*.

He was a stern, intimidating man, with the strong physical presence of a bricklayer. He rarely smiled and took his role as guardian of the *zawiya* very seriously. He was always exacting about where you made ritual ablution and that you wore flip-flops in the toilet; small things. I can't say that I ever got to know him well but I suspect that when he was young he had a hot temper. You could see traces of it in his personality but what was significant was that his personality had been almost completely transmuted by the act of remembrance. Someone described him as rock candy. He was very hard on the outside but very sweet on the inside.

The last time I saw him was in 1981. I had arrived in Rabat on a flight from New York and, passing through immigration, came upon an American couple having trouble at passport control. The U.S. had just changed the size of passports. The passport officer had never seen the new passport size and was refusing to let them in. They were very panicky, so I spoke to the official in Arabic and explained the change and he let them through. They were eternally grateful and, as it happened, we were staying in the same hotel.

They offered to give me a lift to Meknes and Fes, where I was headed. In Meknes I had them leave me off at the *zawiya* and spent the day with the *fuqara*.

Sidi l'Ayyashi was still watching over the *zawiya* with unswerving devotion and caring for the widows of Ibn Al-Habib who lived there. He was very elderly by this time and, if I remember correctly, having trouble seeing. Still, conditioned by my early days as a novice, I was intimidated by this severe, ascetic Sufi.

When the American couple arrived in their car to pick me up, all the old *fuqara* in the *zawiya*, including Sidi l'Ayyashi, came out to the street to see me off. These were men who had turned their backs on the world and spent their lives remembering God, "standing, sitting and reclining". They were the sanest people I knew. They could not have been further removed from the two naïve and slightly goofy New York tourists sitting in their rental car parked across from the *zawiya*.

At the car I said my farewells to these men and climbed in the back seat. I looked out at this cluster of old men and found them leaning in to the windows and greeting the American couple. Suddenly, I saw them through the innocent eyes of these uninitiated tourists. They could have walked straight out of another century, these big hearted, half-blind, gnarled, limping, bearded men, leaning on their walking sticks, in their worn out *djellabas*, huge warm smiles - anachronisms. At the center of the group leaning through the windows and shaking hands with the Americans and with a wide, genial smile was Sidi l'Ayyashi, this imposing presence I had always been a little afraid of.

When we drove away, the Americans were in a state of near hysterical euphoria. "Wow! Incredible! This is the greatest thing that has ever happened to me! I'll never forget this!" All the way to the spa town of Moulay Ya'coub, where we were headed to take the waters, my companions rhapsodized about the men they met.

I can't say how long this memory lasted for them but, for me, the stonemason's radiant face at the window is indelible, the shining badge of a simple life transformed through the alchemy of knowledge, devotion, hard work, service and the constant remembrance of God.

"Know, my son, that God will honor you with sweet and pleasant waters."

I said, "Are these the waters of Islam, Iman and Ihsan?"

He said to me, "They are".

I said, "O Messenger of God, shall I alone drink these waters, or myself and whoever follows me?"

He said, "You and all who follow you of my community shall drink them."

A visionary exchange between the Prophet Mohamed, peace be upon him, and Shaykh Mohamed ibn Al-Habib, may God be well pleased with him*

---

* The Diwan of Mohamed ibn Al-Habib, the Introduction..

ALMOND MILK

If you didn't know anything about him and met him in a dark alley at night, you'd probably start shaking with fear, raise your hands, beg for mercy and hand over your wallet. He was tall, scarred and scary. I forget his name but remember his hard face.

He was, in fact, the polar opposite of this menacing thuggish figure. He was a feature of the bazaars and markets of Fes, patrolling the stalls to make sure both traders and customers behaved themselves. He settled disputes, chased down thieves and pickpockets and generally kept everybody honest. He was like an ex-officio *Muhtasib* or *Sahib Al-Souq*, which in traditional Muslim society was the Keeper of Markets and Public Morality. He didn't get paid for doing this and his role was without any legal basis, but he didn't need a license. His tough, intimidating presence and moral authority were enough. His real life was away from the bazaars, in circles of remembrance. Here he blended in with the motley crowd of Sufis and submerged himself in the Names of God.

Whenever we would come to Fes, we would escape from the rigors of the Way to indulge ourselves in almond milk at a little almond milk bar frequented by Fesi students. The milk bar was on the second level above a bakery just up the cobbled passage from an entrance to the Qarawiyyin Mosque with glass windows that looked out upon the street below. Students would gather in this brightly lit and garish hangout. Young Moroccan couples stared dreamily across the tables over sweet almond milk and biscuits. It was an early breach of the pristine traditional integrity of the ancient city, but for those of us from the West it was an innocent enough diversion and a fleeting relief from the punishing intensity of spiritual discipline, which could be brutally heavy on our over-pampered personalities.

One afternoon a friend and I were coming away from a gathering of invocation and on the way to another when we decided to take a quick, surreptitious detour to the almond milk bar.

We ascended the spiral staircase to the second floor, sat down at a table beside the glass window and sipped the richly sweet infusion. We were in high spirits... until we looked down at the street below and saw the tall, scary *faqir* staring up at us, frowning. All our levity evaporated when, to our dismay, he charged up the stairs and into the almond milk bar.

"What are you doing here?" he snapped, shaking his head. Suddenly, through this powerful *faqir's* eyes, the innocent almond milk bar seemed like an utterly depraved den of iniquity. He shook his head in disgust. "Come on, get up. You're coming with me!" He dragged us away from our almond milk, down the stairs, into the streets and to our next circle of remembrance. "Don't let me *ever* catch you in that place again," he scolded. I never went back there. God bless him and have mercy on him.

"The act of worship that is most beloved to Me is giving good counsel."

Hadith Qudsi*

---

* *Mishkat al-anwar* of Ibn 'Arabi, translated by Stephen Hirtenstein and Martin Notcutt..

ENCOUNTERS

**"Outwardly, creatures are an illusion;
But, inwardly, they are an admonition.
Thus, the soul looks at the illusory exterior
While the heart looks at the admonitory interior."**

Ibn Ata'illah Al-Iskandari*

* *Al-Hikam* translated by Victor Danner.

THE MAN WHO WANTED TO GO TO MADINAH

When I first arrived in Makkah I kept company with a friend from America who was living with his wife close to the Holy Mosque and studying Arabic at Umm Al-Qurra University. One day during Ramadan he mentioned that he had given money to a poor man to visit the mosque and tomb of the Prophet Mohamed, peace and blessings be upon him, in Al-Madinah Al-Munawwwara.

When he said this I thought, "What a wonderful thing to do – to send someone to Madinah. I wish I could do that." For some reason I can't explain I developed an overpowering desire to send someone to visit the Prophet. I didn't mention this to anyone but loved the idea of doing it and kept thinking about it.

A few days later, I made the lesser pilgrimage (*umrah*) after the night prayer with a friend from England. When we finished our rituals, we were relaxing in a circle in the *mataf* between the Yemeni corner and the Black Stone.

While we were sitting, a man approached our circle. He sat down across the circle from me between two of our companions. Clearly, he was looking for a handout. He asked the group something. I wasn't paying much attention and, in fact, found his intrusion annoying. I looked across without much interest and asked what he wanted and my friends told me he wanted alms (*sadaqa*). As I had my money rolled up in my *ihram* and difficult to get to, I made no move to give him anything. All the others reached for their purses or wallets. It was Ramadan after all and a blessed time for giving.

But the man stopped them and called across to me. Pointing to me, he said, "No, him!" I looked up, nonplussed. "You!" he said. I felt embarrassed because I had no intention of giving anything to this fellow. Then he looked me straight in the eye and said, nodding with a meaningful grin, "I want to go to Madinah!" With a jolt of recognition, I unrolled my *ihram* and pulled out the bus fare to Al-Madinah. He took it, refused anything from the others and disappeared.

"No deed is more fruitful for the heart than the one you are not aware of and which is deemed paltry by you."

Ibn Ata'illah Al-Iskandari*

* *Al-Hikam*, translated by Victor Danner.

ALL NIGHT LONG

Sufi Abdallah cut a striking figure. He was a tall, handsome, powerfully built Pathan with an easy swagger, thick salt and pepper beard, a rakish smile and piercing eyes. It was said he worked sixteen hours a day – two consecutive shifts – as a shop foreman in a Birmingham factory. It was also said that he rarely slept, although I had trouble believing this. He led a Naqshbandi Sufi order in Birmingham.

The Naqshbandiyya trace their lineage directly back to our Master Abu Bakr Al-Siddiq, may God be well pleased with him, and their practice, reflecting the quiescence of their spiritual father, was inward and silent. It has been said that the Naqshbandiyya preserved Islam throughout the Central Asian republics during the repressively atheistic Soviet period because their spiritual practice could be carried out in silence, invisibly, without a trace.

The Naqshbandis of Birmingham were anything but invisible. They were a flamboyant, vigorous bunch, mostly working class Pakistani emigrants who congregated with a wonderful sense of processional solidarity behind their towering, energetic leader, arriving at gatherings like the *Eid* prayers by the busload, brandishing banners and flags and carrying trays groaning with Pakistani food. They were far and away the most organized group of Sufis in Britain.

I was always impressed by Sufi Abdallah and the men around him but wondered whether theirs was a case of style over substance. I had my chance to find out when a few friends and I were invited to attend a night of *dhikr* in London. We gathered at a modest brick row house in a working class neighborhood after sunset. We had tea and talked casually until the night prayer, after which a delicious Pakistani supper was served on tablecloths spread across the floor of the room we had gathered in. This seemed more like a social gathering and I began to think my suspicions about these Naqshbandiyya were justified.

For us a meal after the night prayer usually signaled the end of an evening. These men, I discovered, were just getting started. A large circle was formed and the invocation began. The practice of the Naqshbandiyya revolved around the silent invocation of *La ilaha illa 'llah* - "No god but God" - on the breath and with a rhythmic movement of the head down on the "*La*" and the "*illa*" and in a circular motion accompanied by a visualization of light. Although silent, it is an incredibly powerful practice.

Sufi Abdallah led the assembly with single-minded intensity. The practice began slowly and accelerated gradually in unison until the group breathed as a single body, lost in remembrance. Time passed. We were swept away in this luminous circular breath. Time flowed. The invocation ended. It was dawn.

We prayed the dawn prayer and the assembly broke up. I staggered out into the early morning air, ready to collapse. Sufi Abdallah walked out with me. On the working class street he looked down at me with a twinkle in his eye and a chuckle and gave me a pat on the back with his large hand, as if to say, "Nice try". He shook my hand with an iron grip. Unruffled, he was ready to head back to Birmingham to start his first shift. As we parted ways in the cold morning light, I realized that I had just experienced a case of substance over style.

**"Our abode is transitory,
our life therein is but a loan,
our breaths are numbered,
and our indolence is manifest."**

Sayyidina Abu Bakr Al-Siddiq*

* *Kashf Al-Mahjub* by Ali Uthman Al-Hujwiri, translated by Reynold A. Nicholson.

THE WEEPING EYE

A hard rain drenched us as we made our way to the great mosque of Meknes amongst a group of Sufis that had gathered that day for the celebration of the Birth of the Noble Prophet (*Mawlid An-Nabawi Sharif*). Sufis from Morocco and Algeria had converged for the occasion. Moving with the crowd, *djellaba* hood covering my head against the rain, breathing in the pungent smell of wet wool, I was overtaken with the exalted sense of need and longing. I was surrounded by men for whom life in the world had no value but to remember the Lord of Creation. The rain reminded me of tears. I began to weep. The crowd stopped in a passageway leading to the Great Mosque. A *faqir* turned back to face me. He was also in tears but I saw that his tear ducts were distended, gaping open from constant weeping. He looked me in the eyes and pointed to the heavens. Then he turned his back to me and moved forward with the group.

**"It is with a stricken heart
and anguished soul
That, in longing for You,
I rain tears like a cloud."**

Faridu'd-Din 'Attar*

---

* The Speech of the Birds (*Mantiqu't-Tair*), translated by Peter Avery.

THE GLANCE

Pir Aftab came to visit us in London. A spiritual master of a Naqshbandi Sufi order from Pakistan, he was sweet and cherubic with a thick black beard and turban. My heart was in a state of contraction. I sat at the back of the gathering, head lowered. He gave a discourse. I was too distracted with my own self-concerns to listen. My chest was constricted, my eyes burned. I looked up. For one split second, he looked me straight in the eye and smiled. His eye sparked with light. The light hit my heart. My eyes cooled. Peace descended over me. In an instant a crushing weight lifted from me in a single, fleeting glance.

**"People speak of the evil eye
but they overlook the good eye.
The good eye exists.
Just as the one possessed of the evil eye
can cause illness with a glance,
the one possessed of the good eye
can heal with a glance."**

Habib Ahmed Mashhur Al-Haddad*

* Told to the author in conversation.

THE NUBIAN
BESIDE THE TOMB

I landed in Cairo in the summer of 1976 and immediately tried to get a visa to Saudi Arabia. The Saudi Consulate General was, and as of this writing, still is located in Garden City in a huge, run-down complex of buildings. At the time, which was the early years of Saudi Arabia's oil boom, the Embassy was besieged by thousands of visa applicants trying to get into the Kingdom for work or to perform the *Hajj* or *Umrah*.

The heat was oppressive. Crowds surged at the entrance, pushing to get inside the compound. Egyptian police in ill-fitting white uniforms and black berets beat the seething mob back with belts. The heat, the smell of sweating humanity and fumes from the surrounding streets was suffocating. When I finally managed to get through the gates there were incredibly long lines out in the courtyard leading to windows where visa applicants were meant to leave their documents. I was stuck in an interminable queue, which never seemed to get shorter because of new applicants continually cutting in line.

Rather than risk an altercation, I had to resign myself to wait patiently at the back of a long, glacially slow line. Patience is not a virtue I have in large supply but I was stuck without an option. I decided that the only way to make the best of a bad situation was to use the time performing invocation (*dhikru'llah*) and decided to repeat a long form of the Prayer on the Prophet (Al-*Salat 'ala an-Nabi*) 1,000 times. I stood in line for about three hours, sweat streaming down my face, trying not to breathe in the nauseating vapors, damping down my annoyance when yet another queue jumper pushed into the line in front of me, reciting the prayer on the Prophet over and over and over again.

By the time I reached the front of the line, I'd repeated the *dhikr* 990 times and, needless to say, my frustrations and annoyances had gradually been displaced by the repetition of this calming invocation. I deposited my papers at the window and gratefully escaped the Saudi Consulate compound, hailing a taxi to take me to Sayyida Zaynab, the great mosque that encompasses the tomb of the granddaughter of the Prophet Mohamed, may God be pleased with her and may God bless him and give him peace. In the taxi I completed my 1,000th prayer on the Prophet. I paid the driver, got out and entered the Mosque. As I approached the precincts of the tomb of Sayyida Zaynab, an old Nubian *dervish* in a long white shirt and colored turban, sitting beside the tomb, head bowed in invocation, looked up as if he sensed something. He spotted me. His eyes brightened as if he recognized me. He cried out: "*Allah! Allah!*" His hands came up and he pulled them over and over wildly from me toward himself, as if he was trying desperately to gather something unseen from me into his heart. His face was incandescent. I nodded to him. He beamed ecstatically. He then returned to his invocation.

About a week later I entered Sayyida Zaynab again. I had not been performing the prayer on the Prophet or any other form of invocation as intensively as I had that day in the Saudi Consulate. I spotted the Nubian *dervish* and tried to catch his eye. I walked over and sat beside him in front of the tomb. I assumed we had a bond from the week before. He ignored me. When I finally did manage to catch his attention, he looked at me without a glimmer of recognition and returned to his invocations. Whatever he had seen the previous week, it certainly wasn't me. I suspect that he had seen the prayer on the Prophet. But God knows best.

"O Muhammad!
How can we find you here among the ruins?
How can we see you?"

Daniel Abdal-Hayy Moore*

* "Light of the Shadowless One" from *Sparrow on the Prophet's Tomb.*

MEETING WITH
THE MINISTER

I first came to Saudi Arabia to legalize my marriage. My wife and I had been married in a Muslim ceremony in London without knowing that Saudi women had to get official permission to marry foreigners. By the time we found out about this alarming decree, my wife was already pregnant. We tried to find a solution through the Saudi embassy without success. Although we'd intended to settle in Makkah Al-Mukarramah, our suddenly illicit marriage and a child on the way made this idea untenable, to say the least, so after a sojourn in Egypt, we headed West for California where we registered a civil marriage and our first two children were born.

In 1980 I decided to try to sort out our marriage situation, so that my wife could at least return home to see her family. I arrived in Saudi Arabia in the dead of summer and immediately tried finding out how I could go about getting retroactive permission for our illegitimate nuptials. Initial reactions were discouraging. Most people I talked to seemed to think the situation was hopeless. One Saudi industrialist shrugged and said, "You are married in the eyes of God. That is all that is important. Forget about trying to get permission from the authorities." Finally I had some good news when I was introduced to a distinguished Saudi businessman who had served as Minister of Commerce under the late King Faisal. He said, "Of course you can get permission. You have two children. What are they going to do? They won't refuse." He told me exactly how to go about securing permission for our marriage. I was to petition the Minister of Interior, Prince Naif bin Abdul Aziz, or his deputy and younger brother, Prince Ahmed. "I prefer Prince Ahmed," he said. He told me how to write the petition.

The next step was to find a way to reach one or the other of these two eminent and powerful men. Following the advice I was given, I managed to find out how to get to Prince Ahmed's office and the times he would meet petitioners. We turned up and were placed in an anteroom to wait. We waited several hours. Then one of the attendants closed the door to the anteroom and we heard the sound of people passing. Then the door was opened and we were informed that the Prince had left suddenly. It turned out that there had recently been an attempt on his life and he wasn't meeting anyone. Of course no one told us this until after we'd been waiting. The next step was to find a way to reach the Minister of Interior himself.

At that time the summer capital of Saudi Arabia was in Taif and all the government was in the mountain city. My brother-in-law had a friend from Taif who offered to help get me to the Minister. The friend was Bukhari, a Saudi of Central Asian extraction. He was very friendly and well meaning but also a little crazy and I was completely at his mercy. By this time it was Ramadan, the month of fasting, and during the day my new friend regaled me with stories about his sexual fantasies until I had to ask him to stop. When we would get to his house in the afternoons, he would light up a cigarette and eat - just being in his company made me feel like I was breaking my fast.

A kindly Indian professor I met in Jeddah had generously lent me his car to use while he was away on his summer break and my helper from Taif insisted on driving me around the city in it. His driving was as reckless as the rest of his behavior but there was little I could do but ask him to slow down and drive more carefully. We discovered that the Minister received petitions at a weekly gathering (*majlis*) held at the government palace in Taif. We arranged to attend. On the eve of the *majlis*, my Taifi friend took my borrowed car out on an errand... and wrecked it. The whole front end of the Japanese car was smashed in. I had been trying to resolve our marriage situation for months by this time; I was running out of money and had had one setback after another but this was the last straw. I had this ominous feeling that I was in the wrong company in the wrong place at the wrong time and that I was never going to succeed. I normally don't give up easily and am rarely prone to gloom but this episode took all the wind out of my sails. I became utterly and quite openly depressed and discouraged. All I wanted to do was to get out of that place. My guilty friend from Taif tried to cheer me up but I was inconsolable. He insisted I come with him to a breakfast (*iftar*) at the home of one of his friends. It was the last thing I felt like doing but I was staying at his house and couldn't refuse.

We arrived just before the sunset prayer at the gathering of young Saudi men. I was lost in my thoughts. How was I going to explain the car to the Indian professor? How was I going to pay for the repairs, if the car even could be repaired? What if, once again, we couldn't get my petition to the Minister? How much longer was this excruciating process going to take? My wife was stuck in California with our two babies and having a hard time coping. I wasn't earning. How was I going to be able to support them? All these thoughts were running through my head at the fast-breaking. I was oblivious to everything around me.

When the meal was finished, our young host asked me to come with him, for what reason I didn't know. He took me into another room in the house. Here his father was sitting alone. He held prayer beads, which he was working. His face was serene and luminous. His presence was healing. I realized immediately I was in the presence of one of God's rightly-guided servants (*salihin*). He said to me, "My son has told me about your predicament. Your affair is in the hands of your Lord. Remember, these princes, these men are slaves of God. They have no real power. They can only do what God decrees. Put your trust in God and He will take care of you." He then instructed me to recite the formula, *Ya Al-Ali, Al-Khabir* (Oh the Exalted, the Aware) ceaselessly and to recite *Sura Yasin* forty times during the night. When I left his presence my heart had calmed and my spirits had lifted.

I immediately began repeating the invocation he recommended and, when I was alone at night recited *Sura Yasin*. My recitation was slow and halting, so I only managed to recite Sura Yasin half the number he prescribed before setting off for the Ministry of Interior to attend the *majlis* of Prince Naif.

On the way I continued repeating the invocation silently and praying for success. As my wife's official guardian, my brother-in-law accompanied me to present the petition for our marriage. On the ride over to the Ministry he was laughing and joking, but when we reached the *majlis* hall he discovered that what we were doing was no laughing matter.

Petitioners were pushed roughly into a long line. As each petitioner reached the front of the line two very large and powerful mixed blood (*muwalid* – half Arab-half African) guards in white robes carrying holstered guns and bandoliers stepped forward on each side and grabbed his arms so he couldn't move.

Less than a year earlier, the Holy Mosque in Makkah had been seized by fanatics and turned into an armed fortress in an attempt to overthrow the Saudi government. A bloody two-week siege left hundreds dead and the Saudi government badly shaken. Security had been intensified.

My brother-in-law wasn't ready for this degrading procedure and became highly agitated. But I had been reciting Qur'an and invocation all night long and my heart was absolutely tranquil by this time. I was like a dead body in the hands of the guards.

When our turn came, my brother-in-law, his arms pinned to his sides, approached the Minister. I stood two paces behind him similarly constrained. He handed over the petition to an aide who handed it to Prince Naif. My brother-in-law blurted out our situation: that I was an American and married his sister and that we had two children. The Minister looked up puzzled and said "So what's the problem?" My brother-in-law said, "They didn't have official permission." Prince Naif nodded in recognition and looked past my brother-in-law and into my eyes.

Desert sheikhs and princes raised to rule are taught from an early age to read petitioners' faces. They see so many people they have to gauge character in a glance in order to make snap decisions. I learned this from a friend of mine who had been a ruler in Southern Arabia. Our eyes met.

My heart was serene. I looked at him calmly with no fear or emotion of any kind, nodded respectfully and smiled. He "read" me. He smiled back. He then looked to my brother-in-law, gestured to the side, and said, "*Istirih*" ("Take your ease"), which meant that we were to sit to the side and wait. He read the petition carefully and signed it. Our marriage was approved.

A few days later my crazy helper delivered my borrowed car completely repaired, as if nothing had happened. God is the most Generous of the Generous and the Most Merciful of the Merciful.

My brief Ramadan encounter with a simple man of God the night before had turned the tide and transformed what seemed like a hopeless ordeal into an unexpected success. I lived for twenty-three years in the sacred precincts of Makkah, and my compassionate benefactor who came to my rescue and gave me good counsel and a remedy for my disconsolate heart was a pivotal instrument of this incredible blessing. May God reward him and cover him with Mercy.

"O child of Adam, have no fear of one who holds power, when My Power endures permanently. My Power is permanent, and it shall never be depleted."

Hadith Qudsi*

---

* *Mishkat al-anwar* of Ibn 'Arabi, translated by Stephen Hirtenstein and Martin Notcutt.

WORK

Throughout the 1980s I travelled frequently to India on assignment as a travel writer. I was headed back to the subcontinent to begin work on a travel book I was planning. I was to be part of a delegation of travel writers from the U.S., Canada and the U.K. Srinagar was to be one of the stops on our extended itinerary. I mentioned in passing to my Shaykh, Habib Ahmed Mashhur Al-Haddad, may God be well pleased with him, that I was on my way back to Kashmir and he said, "You know there are many great Sufis in Kashmir." I loved Kashmir and had visited there as a travel writer many times over the years but it had never occurred to me to seek out the company of Sufis. This time I made it my intention to make an effort to meet one of the Sufis of Kashmir.

When I landed I made contact with a young friend, Jan Mohamed Koul, a student at the University of Kashmir who lived with his family in a spacious wooden house in a wooded area near Nagin Lake, which was named Koul Wari, after his clan, who had been high caste Hindus that converted to Islam centuries before. I asked him if he could help me find a Sufi and he became excited, exclaiming that his brother was a disciple of one of the great Sufis of Kashmir and that he would try to arrange a meeting. The Pir lived in a village some distance from Srinagar where he was the imam of the local mosque. As part of a press delegation, my schedule was very full and I only managed to find time for the excursion on the day before we were scheduled to fly to Ladakh on the next leg of our tour. We set off for the village in the late-morning and arrived just after the noon prayer. We found the Pir alone in his mosque. I told him that I had come from Makkah and that my Shaykh had inspired me to seek him out. He said to me that he did not conduct what he called "spiritual conversation" until after midnight and asked me to remain in the village until then so that we could meet. I told him that this was impossible; that I had to take a flight at dawn the next day. He said, "As you are from Makkah, I will come down to Srinagar in your honor and we can meet there after midnight."

We returned to the city and I went back to the hotel to pack my bags, prepare for travel and meet with my colleagues. Late at night Jan Mohamed picked me up at the hotel and we made our way to his brother's house where a number of disciples had gathered to meet their master. He greeted me warmly. We drank tea and ate a late night meal. I was full of questions and had anticipated a fascinating "spiritual conversation". Instead, once the meal had been cleared away, the Pir initiated me into the order's core practice. It was like nothing I had ever seen or experienced in classical western Sufism.

It was a meditation reminiscent of a Hindu breathing practice. The Pir had me place my fingers in my ears and press against my eyelids and breathe through my nose. He explained that the exercise focused on the hearing. In the beginning, he said, I would hear the buzzing of bees. Eventually this would be replaced by the ringing of bells. Ultimately, hearing and seeing would merge and the sound would become a light and from the light the Prophet Mohammed, peace and blessings be upon him, would appear. His disciples all looked to me with passionate enthusiasm and shared some of their spiritual experiences that resulted from the practice.

This was all so alien that I felt deeply uncomfortable, but I had asked for the meeting and the Pir had come all the way to Srinagar to accommodate me so I followed his instructions. Lo and behold, when I covered my eyes and began breathing, a powerful sound of buzzing bees filled my ears. I have to admit it was intoxicating. My misgivings receded. He drilled me on the practice for a half an hour or so. Then he said to me: "Can you give me 5 hours a day for this practice?"

I shook my head in disbelief: "Absolutely not!"

He asked, "Can you give me 3 hours a day?"

"Never!"

"Can you give me 2 hours a day?"

"I'm afraid not."

"Can you give me one hour a day?"

I relented doubtfully. "I will try."

Newly initiated, I departed in the early hours of the morning in time for two hours sleep before leaving for the airport and the flight to Ladakh.

In Ladakh, in Delhi and back in Makkah I made a brave attempt to perform this practice as I had promised the Pir. I never again heard the buzzing of bees and, eventually, abandoned the exercise. It was just too strange.

Sometime later I was sitting with my Shaykh Ahmed Mashhour Al-Haddad and a group of his disciples, one of whom was from India, and I mentioned this episode and the practice I'd been initiated into without going into too much detail. I wanted to understand what it was I'd experienced and whether it was authentic.

When I started describing the meditation, a look of consternation passed through the gathering. The disciple from India said reproachfully, "This is a Hindu meditation." Others shook their heads, disapprovingly. I was embarrassed.

Habib listened, frowning intently and without comment. Then, as if a light had been turned on, he said, "I know what this is, Haroon! (my Muslim name) This is *shughul* (work). This is an exercise for disciples who have a lot of time on their hands. You have to spend a lot of time doing this to get results. Haroon, look at you. You are travelling all over the place. You work all the time. You don't have the time for this."

It made perfect sense. The disciples of the Kashmiri Pir were locked away in their homes during the long, snowbound winters. They had weeks and months to work on this meditation. But the practice was legitimate.

A veil of understanding had been lifted through the depth of insight and breadth of knowledge of my Shaykh, may God cover him with Mercy and bless the Kashmiri Pir and all the saints and people on the Way, wherever they may be.

"And make your work (shughlun) the invocation of God..."

Shaykh Mohamed ibn Al-Habib*

---

* The Diwan - "The Greater Song".

PLAY

He would hold informal court every evening between the sunset prayer and the night prayer in the Holy Mosque in Makkah, overlooking the *mataf* between the Yemeni Corner and the Black Stone. Sitting magisterially above the marble stairway leading up to the raised Sinan Pasha Mosque that surrounded the *mataf*, his station was directly beneath the elevated sound booth (*muqabiliyah*) from where the *mu'adhin* would call the prayer. Draped in brilliant white Sudani robes, head wrapped in a flamboyant voluminous turban, his black beard flecked with grey, his handsome face luminous, his smile dazzling, he was an imposing, romantic figure.

Every habitué of the *Haram Sharif* in Makkah knew Shaykh Ismail. He was hard to miss; a magnetic presence, attracting worshippers and seekers of all kinds. One would rest awhile in the pleasure of his company between the prayers. The atmosphere around him was informal, almost playful. I would always greet him when I passed by and would sit with him from time to time.

It was said that he knew the sciences of the unseen and sometimes cured those afflicted by mental illnesses, possession and magic. He was among the few who the conservative religious authorities allowed to openly practice this science, even though his Sufism was anathema to them.

If I remember correctly, he was a Shaykh of the Idrissi Order in Sudan. He lived across from the *Souq Al-Lail* in a simple flat on Gazah Street. He had students and the occasional patient and spent his days in worship and study.

On one occasion I introduced the Shaykh to a group of visitors from the U.S. He invited us to his home for supper after the night prayer. Several members of the group were Shia Muslims. Although a Sunni, Shaykh Ismail spoke with great learning on Shia doctrine, mentioning that whereas Sufism evolved as a sep-

71

arate strand within Sunni Islam that Sufism is completely integrated into Shia canonic law (*Shariah*). One of the most striking characteristics of the great Sufi scholars I have been able to meet is their inclusiveness and acceptance of all professions within Islam.

On the other hand, hypocrisy, falsehood and lying are universally condemned. He once told me, apropos of nothing in particular at the time, "The worst human being on earth is the man of false claims. There is nothing worse than this." He added further that anyone who openly claimed to be a shaykh, in the sense of being a spiritual master, was automatically a liar.

We were sitting together after the sunset prayer. He knew I was from America but nothing more. He began to ask me about myself. I told him that I was of Arab extraction but had been orphaned as an infant and never knew my birth parents. I was not raised as a Muslim but had embraced Islam as a young adult. He asked me if my birth father was a Muslim. I told him that I knew he was from Syria but had always assumed that he was Christian because many Syrian Christians emigrated from Syria and settled in America in the years after the First World War.

When I said this, Shaykh Ismail reached over and placed the fingers of his right hand on my throat, just above my esophagus, touching my jugular vein. He closed his eyes and with his outspread hand touching my throat, he recited an invocation for a long time. When he finished, he took his hand away, flashed a huge smile and said emphatically, "Your father was a Muslim. His father was a Muslim. His father was a Muslim and *his* father was a Muslim!"

I walked away from this encounter skeptical, to say the least. I am wary of spiritual guides who resort to theatrical gestures of this sort. I didn't give much thought or credence to the exchange but later on, mostly to satisfy my curiosity, I asked my shaykh Sayyid Omar Abdullah to come with me to the Holy Mosque to meet Shaykh Ismail. I told Sayyid Omar about the previous exchange I'd had and I wanted his insight.

After the sunset prayer I led Sayyid Omar to Shaykh Ismail's *maqam* (his established place in the mosque). When Shaykh Ismail saw him approaching with me he cried out *"Abshir! Abshir!"* (Good news! Good news!), as if he was greeting a dear long-lost friend. The two men sat together and spoke at length, thoroughly enjoying one another's company. When we left Shaykh Ismail's circle, and descended the marble stairs to cross the *mataf*, I asked Sayyid Omar what he made of the Sudanese shaykh. Sayyid Omar shook his head with awe. "He is *Wasil*," he said. "He has arrived. He is so advanced that he can play. His knowledge is very, very great."

There is a saying, "Blood will tell" (*al 'iraq dassas*). It seems my blood told Shaykh Ismail a story. But God knows best.

"The Wasil (those joined to God)...are perfect. The Wasil are those near to God (Muqarrab) and those gone before others (Sabiq) in faith."

Shaykh Shahab-u'd-din As-Suhrawardi*

---

* *Awarif Al-Ma'arif*, translated by Wilberforce Clark.

THE LORD OF
THE MIDDLE ATLAS

I led a small group to a settlement in the Middle Atlas in Morocco to learn horsemanship and the *hadra* (sacred dance) from a group of Berber *fuqara* from a branch of the Darqawiyya Sufi order famed for their equestrian skills, descendents of the fearless riders depicted by Delacroix in the 19th century. The fathers and grandfathers of many of these men had fought the French occupation during the colonial period and had left a rough and ready legacy of Sufi practice. We took a bus from Khenifra to a small town called Zawiya Sheikh. We then set out on foot for the settlement of Sidi Saleh, built upon a plateau in the foothills of the Middle Atlas. We arrived unannounced after sundown. We came upon a simple long building from which the droning sound of a Sufi litany (*wird*) could be heard in progress. We entered the large room. A circle of men, most of very advanced years, several blind, scarred or missing limbs, sat on the far left of the room.

I was acutely aware that we were uninvited guests and wanted to give the best possible impression. When we entered the *zawiya* we immediately approached the *fuqara* and passed swiftly counter-clockwise around the circle, kissing each *faqir's* right hand in the traditional greeting. We then moved as a group to the far side of the *zawiya* to make two cycles of prayer to greet the mosque and then completed our sunset prayers. I glanced over at the circle and saw that the old *fuqara* were nodding to each other in approval of our observance of the *Sunna* and Sufi protocols. We then joined the recitation of the *wird*.

Stepping into their circle of *dhikr* was like stepping into a time warp. One was transported to another century. The modern world seemed far removed from the lives of these gnarled, weather-beaten Berbers. Traditionally most *awrad* take between ten to forty minutes to complete. The *wird* these men recited took nearly 3 hours and they recited with great speed. When the *wird* was finally completed, the assembly rose and performed the night prayer. After the prayer I was able to introduce our small company. The conversation was pleasant and desultory. We'd been sitting for several hours already and everything seemed so inconclusive. Were we to be welcomed and put up for the night? Did these men have supper? Nothing seemed to be happening.

One member of our group was a precocious, funny and incredibly handsome young boy of about 11 years old whose mother was a formidable woman with a great heart and piercing intelligence. Hasan was like the barometer of the group. He kept looking at me as if to say, *"What's going on here?"* We waited patiently. I was beginning to think that we were going to have to traipse back down the mountain in the dead of night and find someplace else to stay. Finally, after another hour or so, a young boy beckoned us to follow him. We went outside the *zawiya* and were taken around to the back of the building, which was a long room identical to the front half of the structure.

Standing to one side of the room was the strange, majestic figure of Sidi Saleh, the founder of his eponymous community, the shaykh of this extraordinary Sufi order and spiritual lord of the Middle Atlas. He was an incredibly romantic figure, conjuring images of Orson Welles in "The Black Rose". His most striking feature was his huge, oriental, kohl-laden eyes. His face was luminous and quite beautiful but also slightly odd. He moved with the languid ease and authority of a king, which, I suppose, is close to what he was in this district, yet his gestures had a jerky quality that I attributed to his mountain Berber upbringing. He welcomed us warmly. We sat and, finally, were served milky coffee and Moroccan biscuits.

I told him that we'd been sent to learn horsemanship and the sacred dance, the *hadra* (also called *imara*) of his Sufi order. The moment I mentioned *"imara"*, Sidi Saleh's eyes lit up, he clapped his hands twice and, suddenly, the entire assembly of about 30 men leapt to their feet, formed a huge circle and instantaneously began the most extraordinary *hadra* I have ever seen or experienced. It was a complex and pulsating dance with an incredible double bounce. To use the parlance of my American generation, it rocked.

Young Hasan was in the circle with us. On the outside of the circle children about his age or younger gathered. They were a strange looking collection, many with their heads shaved, presumably against lice, but with tufts of hair left intact, sticking out in odd places from their bald scalps, apparently a pre-Islamic Berber custom. These children, eyes closed, were swaying and rocking and bouncing at the back of the circle. It was an utterly bizarre sight. I glanced over at Hasan who was looking at these rapturous rocking children with wide-eyed wonder.

When the *hadra* was over, we were all reeling, intoxicated and exhausted. And then a magnificent feast was served; a sheep upon a huge bed of couscous garnished with fresh vegetables. While we were eating, bathed in the illuminated backwash of the *hadra*, it dawned on me why we'd been waiting for hours. When we arrived unannounced, Sidi Saleh had ordered that a sheep be slaughtered and a feast prepared in our honor.

With this overwhelming reception, Sidi Saleh ordered his *fuqara* to make us comfortable in the *zawiya*. We were all given mattresses to sleep on and a vast Berber *hanafiya* carpet was draped over us all to serve as a single, expansive blanket against the frigid mountain air.

The people of Sidi Saleh had withdrawn from the world into their haven of sanity. One only had to travel down to the tawdry village of Zawiya Sheikh to understand what they were escaping from. They spoke a patois of Shilha, the Berber dialect, Arabic and a smattering of French. They were living a life that revolved around the remembrance of God.

At dawn we were awakened. We made *wudhu* and prayed the dawn prayer after which the litany began. Again, it lasted for hours, until long after sunrise. I calculated that the *awrad* alone these men recited took up about six hours of every day.

We then had breakfast, which consisted of freshly baked bread and freshly pressed olive oil from the orchards that surrounded the village. The cold pressed olive oil was like a meal in itself. It was the finest olive oil I have ever tasted and upon my departure I took away a bottle of this nectar with me.

The morning was languorous. Some of the younger men set up piles of stones and threw other stones at them to dislodge the piles. They played this aimless game for hours. I asked about the possibility of learning horsemanship from these famed riders, but was told that their horses were out to pasture.

On the morning of the first day, I was driven down the hill to Zawiya Shaikh to pay the obligatory visit to the *qaid*, the district head-man. These visits were necessary in those days to reassure the local authorities that there was nothing subversive in visits from foreigners. At the time Moroccans had to carry an official *laissez-passeré* to travel outside their home districts. I resented being taken away from the sanctity of Sidi Saleh to be interrogated by the official but knew that this protected the community from what could be an intrusive police inquisition. I walked in with a chip on my shoulder. While the *qaid* was not exactly wreathed in a halo, he was also not a particularly objectionable character. He looked at me with an amused smile. Arrogant and hotheaded American that I was, I upbraided him for dragging me down the hill for interrogation. He was patient, asked me a few questions and, seemingly satisfied that I was harmless, excused me and sent me on my way back up the hill.

After the noon prayer we were once again feasted. No one seemed to work in this village. Yet we were eating like kings. I was curious. I asked one of the *fuqara* how much land they owned. His arm swept across the panoramic view of the plains which stretched out from the foothills as far as the eye could see. He smiled and said, "Everything you see!"

So that was it. They were incredibly wealthy but eccentric landowners, agricultural barons.

I later learned that they had nothing. The younger men worked harvesting crops. Some left to work in the cities. In times of dearth they would sometimes go for weeks living off bread and oil. The feasts we were treated to were from the colossal hospitality of these generous Berbers who went out among their community to find the provisions to feed us.

Several of the younger men were assigned to take care of us. One of these men was a deaf-mute, a lovely young man, very innocent, with the awkwardness and dislocation of the hearing impaired. He performed the *hadra* with incredible focus and skill, which I thought extraordinary given that he couldn't hear anything. We took walks up in the foothills above the village. Sidi Saleh had founded the community as a refuge for his disciples from the depredations and depravities of modern life. Living was primitive and civilized at the same time. Connections with the outside world were tenuous. The views across the plains were breathtaking. I'm not sure the experiment was altogether successful. The pull of the world was very strong and many of the younger men left the community for the seductions of the city.

I became friendly with their Imam, Sidi Abdul Rahman, a robust man of about 40 years of age. He invited me into his home, which was among a cluster of small buildings set at a distance from the central *zawiya* hall and the lodgings of Sidi Saleh. His home was a simple rectangular room divided by a sheet. He had two wives. One wife lived on one side of the sheet and the other lived on the other side of the sheet. From all appearances they lived in domestic harmony.

We stayed three days as guests of Sidi Saleh, in accordance with the rules of travel. When I announced that we would be leaving on the third day, Sidi Saleh came out and insisted that we stay on for at least *three more weeks*! He had plans for us. He wanted us to travel with him. He had already worked out the itinerary. I thanked him and told him that we really did have to make our way back to Meknes. Sidi Saleh looked stricken, as if he really needed us to stay with him. I have to say I wavered, genuinely tempted to abandon our schedule and take to the road with this wonderful man. But I was responsible for getting our group back to base at the right time. I had to decline. When it became clear that there was no way he could convince us to travel with him, Sidi Saleh handed me a fist full of dirhams and sent us with his blessing on our way down the hill.

May God bless his memory and have mercy on him and all those who followed him.

**"Renunciation is to look at the world,
keeping in mind that it is passing,
in order that it be diminished in your eyes,
thus making it easy for you to turn away from it."**

Ibn Jalaa*

* From the Epistle of Qushayri, included in Realities of Sufism by Shaykh Abd Al-Qadir Isa, transated by Suraqah Abdul Aziz.

THE UNSEEN

Bashir Othman lived in Al-Madinah Al-Munawwara and was among the sacred city's greatest men of God. He was from Eritrea and was a disciple of the great Eritrean Shaykh Mohamed Abu Bakr. He guided many on the Sufi way. I didn't know him well, although several of my friends were his students. He knew the sciences of the unseen and healed those afflicted with possession and illnesses resulting from black magic.

One day he honored me with a visit to my home in Makkah. At that time I was writing a newspaper column on film and spending rather more time than I should have looking at movies. I was concerned about this and asked him how dangerous it was to watch movies, which more conservative Muslims considered to be completely forbidden. His answer surprised me. He said, "What you hear has more impact on the spirit than what you see. The auditory is more powerful than the visual. Beware of what you listen to."

He then initiated me into the invocation *Ya Latif,* which he prescribed to be repeated many thousands of times every night. He said, "If you recite this invocation, the unseen will be unveiled for you."

I mentioned this to my shaykh Sayyid Omar Abdullah, may God be well pleased with him. He laughed, shook his head and said, "Don't do it."

I said, "I had a feeling you'd say this. I have enough trouble with the seen world. I don't think I'm ready for the unseen, right?"

Sayyid Omar laughed again, nodded this time, and said, "Right."

"The perfect meaning of Al-Latif combines gentleness in action with delicacy of perception."

Imam Abu Hamid Al-Ghazali*

* The Ninety-Nine Beautiful Names of God (*al-Maqsad al-asna fi sharh asma' Allah al-husna*), translated by David B. Burrell and Nazih Daher.

THE ILLUMINATED

**"The religion of God is light.
His Book is light.
His Messenger is light.
The abode which He has prepared
for His intimate friends glows with light.
God is the light of the heavens and the earth;
one of His Names is Light."**

Ibn Qayyim Al Jawziyya*

---

* *Al-Wabil al-Sayyib min al-Kalim al Tayyib* ("The Invocation of God") translated by Michael Abdurrahman Fitzgerald and Moulay Youssef Slitine.

Photo left: Shaykh Mohamed ibn Al-Habib

FIRST LIGHT

He was one of the most beautiful men I have ever laid eyes on, physically and spiritually. I first met Moulay Abu'l Qasim in Meknes in 1973 during the *Moussem* of Shaykh Mohamed ibn Al-Habib. We had arrived in a caravan from England and settled in to a small courtyard house in the valley below the *zawiya* of the Shaykh. When we entered the *zawiya* for the first time, we proceeded straight to the circle of Sufis in the corner of the room, all sitting silently invoking God. I joined my companions who were more experienced than I, moving round the circle of men counter-clockwise, kissing each man's hand. Most of the *fuqara* were over 60 years of age. All greeted us warmly.

I proceeded around the circle until I came to a man swathed in white with his head lowered in meditation, sitting against the *qibla* wall. He was simply one man in a circle of many but when he raised his head to return my greeting I was dazzled by the extreme beauty of his face. His smile was like a sun. His features were sharp, his nose wide and hawk-like. He was about 70 years old at the time I met him but looked ageless. He could have been 40. I almost swooned at the sight of him. His presence was overpowering. His whole being was effulgent. I didn't know anything about him at the time but I immediately recognized his holiness. He was the first Sufi saint I recognized. I became very attached to this man and thought of him frequently.

During my visits to Morocco I would try to sit beside him. I did not, however, feel worthy of his company and was far too intimidated by his presence to do more than seek physical proximity to him. His voice was as beautiful as his face – soft, broken and ethereal – permeated with intimacy. He spoke very little and when he did, he spoke only of Paradise and God's love of His creatures. On one occasion, he addressed us, saying with quiet, emphatic certainty, "This gathering is in Paradise". I am, by nature, skeptical of theatrics or theatrical statements like this, but the atmosphere was so transfigured by his presence, infused as it was with remembrance of the Divine, that he seemed to be stating the obvious. I remember he once said, "There is nothing on earth that God loves more than His slave, hands raised helplessly in supplication, weeping, and pleading."

On certain occasions he would sing *qasa'id*, sometimes while leading a *hadra*. His voice was unearthly, the most celestial voice I have ever heard, as if the song he sang was emanating from the ethers; he seemed never to take a breath. In the center of a *hadra* he had the grace of a leopard. At the end of a *hadra* his eyes brimmed with tears, his heart heaved, as if he had been sucked into a vortex of luminous divinity and returned absorbed in an indescribable passion. He was the first human being that gave me certainty of the Path. He was a proof of the vibrant reality of Islam for me and his memory has kept me within the Way for 40 years. He combined all the aspects of a Man of God – sobriety, intoxication, serenity, compassion, subtlety, love, knowledge, wisdom, humility and strength.

For all his gentleness and he was one of the gentlest men I have ever encountered, he could be fierce. One afternoon during a meal, I watched him closely. He ate very little – three balls of couscous – during a meal. However, it was almost impossible to recognize this. Had I not been following his every move, I would have assumed he was eating as heartily as the rest of those at the table. There was nothing ostentatious about his abstinence. I had observed that he always passed food to whoever sat to his right. This was a practice of the Prophet Mohamed, may God bless him and give him peace. The *adab*, or spiritual courtesy, in response to such an action is to accept any food offered, particularly by an elder. Whenever I was able to sit to his right hand side during a meal, I eagerly took the bread he passed to me. On this occasion, toward the end of the meal, he passed some bread to the *faqir* on his right hand. This *faqir* was dominating the table talk. In the aftermath of the *hadra*, an intoxicating lightness pervades the atmosphere and it is very easy to allow levity to overtake the sobriety of the act of remembrance. The man on his right hand was a little carried away and talking too much. When the bread was passed to him, he pushed it back to Moulay Abu'l Qasim, pointing to his stomach, saying something to the effect that he had eaten enough and couldn't possibly have more. He was being polite but he was, in the context of the gathering, behaving with a lack of *adab*. I paid close attention to Moulay Abu'l Qassim. He looked at the bread and moved it back in front of his neighbor. The man continued his conversation, smiled and insisted that he really couldn't take the bread. He pushed it back. Moulay Abu'l Qasim looked silently at the bread for a moment and in one powerful motion, grabbed his neighbor's wrist, lifted his arm, put the bread in the man's hand and closed his fingers over it, staring fiercely into his eyes. He then quietly resumed eating, leaving the fellow stunned and with a powerful lesson in the small spiritual courtesies of Sufism, which lie at the core of the practice.

When I returned to the West I began to dream of Moulay Abu'l Qasim. These dreams were all slightly strange. In one dream I was in a cinema, watching a film and he entered and sat down behind me. In another I was in a gymnasium and he walked through the locker room, nodding to me. I puzzled over these strange appearances until I learned that he had been ordered by the Shaykh to watch over those of us from the West. It occurred to me that his appearances in unlikely settings may have been a reminder to remember God in every time and place.

One from among our group contracted a virulent case of dysentery while in Morocco. He became emaciated and was extremely ill for many days. Moulay Abu'l Qasim turned up at the door of the small courtyard house where we were staying unannounced and asked to see the man who was ill. He sat beside him and asked for a glass of water. He put his right forefinger into the glass and recited from the Qur'an. He gave the man the water to drink. Then he took his leave. Before he departed he told us, "He will have one more attack and then he will be all right." And this is what happened.

I always tried to sit as close to Moulay Abu'l Qasim as I possibly could. From a distance he was a dazzling figure, wreathed in light, which was enhanced by his white *burnoose*, green turban and spotless white *haik* (head-cover). His carriage, his appearance, was that of a prince, and indeed he was. Yet at close quarters I noticed that his garments had been patched and mended in dozens of places – holes that had been meticulously stitched. When he entered the *zawiya* and slipped out of his shoes, I noticed that they were completely worn out, falling apart. Yet, there was no indication at all that he was poor. He was truly the wealthiest man I have ever encountered.

**"Roam around these tents for evermore,
Drink the cups that hold the wine of love;
Cast off all others, have courtesy,
At this station, where there's none above.
In Contemplation's Presence there's a wine
Which strips all lovers of the joy of sleep.
In Contemplation's Presence there's a wine
Which leads a thirsty passion ocean deep."**

Al-Habib al-Imam Ali ibn Muhammad Al-Habshi*

* From Key to the Garden by Habib Ahmad Mashhur Al-Haddad, translated by Mostafa Al Badawi.

BLACK LIGHT

He was a rugged one-eyed black man who looked a little like a buccaneer. He wore the dark green turban of the Darqawiyya and a ragged coarse wool *djellaba*. He had large calloused hands, a virile, commanding presence and he walked with a swagger. His gestures were abrupt and powerful. He had a radiant grin. His rough appearance belied a profound spirituality. He was utterly devoted to the act of remembrance and had the Name of God on his lips at all times, even when he slept. One of us came upon him when he was fast asleep. With every exhalation of breath he sighed, *"Allllaaaah"*. When he was awake, he worked his prayer beads ceaselessly. He was meticulous in his observance of the prayers and the times of *dhikr*. To keep time he carried around a large alarm clock in his *djellaba*, which he would pull out and squint at as if it were a pocket watch.

He lived in the most impoverished slum outside the walls of Meknes, a sprawling shantytown called the Borj. The Borj was a vast dilapidated exurb of wooden hovels covered by corrugated iron and tin roofing. The mosque was a rickety wooden hall with a makeshift minaret formed of old tin scraps riveted together.

From here he presided over the *dhikr* of the Habibiyya Order as the *muqaddam*, or deputy, of the Shaykh. I never knew his name. We always knew him as the Muqaddam of the Borj. In honor of the poor, the Shaykh, may God be well pleased with him, always held his *Moussem* (annual spiritual celebration) in the Borj. The Muqaddam of the Borj hosted hundreds of *fuqara* congregating in his ramshackle *zawiya* to remember God and praise the Prophet Mohamed, peace and blessings be upon him. He moved through the gathering with great authority. His *fuqara* were among the most impressive in the order. It was the greatest night in the year for these men. The *zawiya* pulsated with invocation. The *hadra* was always overpowering.

In 1986 I visited Morocco as a guest of the Moroccan tourism authority. Once my work was done I made my way to Meknes and the *zawiya*. The *fuqara* were very polite and pleased that I could recite the entire *wird* of the Ibn Al-Habib from memory, but there was a reserve I wasn't accustomed to. One afternoon, as we were sitting around a tray of food eating lunch, the Muqaddam of the Borj casually asked me about a disciple who had claimed to be a spiritual master. He asked me point blank what I thought of him. All the *fuqara* looked at me intently. Surprised, I paused and then said carefully, "I believe that he is very far from the Path." Suddenly, the ice was broken, the group relaxed and burst out laughing. The Muqaddam of the Borj slapped me on the knee, patted my back and, beamed, nodding vigorously. They had accepted me as one of their own and we launched into a round of invocation to seal the moment. This was the last occasion I saw this magnificent illuminated guardian of the poorest of the poor.

"Let me live among the poor, die among the poor and be raised up among the poor."

The Messenger of God*

*Tirmidhi and Bayhaqi, in *Shu'ab al-Iman.*

THE BEACON

I was with a group trudging up one of the long steep cobbled streets of the ancient city of Fes. The streets were teeming at that time of day. Crowds of pedestrians were walking down the hill in our direction. Far away up the hill in the distance I saw a shining light, from a face in the crowd, like a beacon. I couldn't make out the features, the distance was too great, but I became transfixed by this dazzling light moving down the hill through the crowds. My heart was pounding. I had never seen anyone so radiant. I watched this slow-approaching figure bathed in supernal light with anticipation and rising excitement. When he came closer I was stunned. The illuminated figure I had been watching was a man I already knew, someone who I always associated with severity and scholarship. His formal knowledge veiled his hidden illumination. He knew us. He beamed and shook my hand with a powerful grip before moving on down the hill.

The first time I saw Si Fudul Al-Hawari Al-Sufi was shortly after I had entered the Path. I attended a gathering of *fuqara* in the city of Meknes at the elegant home of Moulay Hashem Balghiti, who has since become the Shaykh of the Habibiyya Order. The *hadra* was held in the open courtyard of the large house. The *fuqara* sang from the *Diwan* of Shaykh Mohamed ibn Al-Habib and, as evening moved into night the recitation of the *Diwan* gave way to the sacred dance. The *hadra* was powerful and induced intense concentration in the gathering. Upon its completion, an austere and unassuming scholar began to give a discourse. At the time I didn't speak a word of Arabic but a companion whispered what it was about. The discourse was on the most prosaic of subjects, the act of *wudhu*, or ritual ablution. The scholar's presentation was soft spoken, simple and matter-of-fact. He began by going through the process of *wudhu*, step by step, explaining the deeper meaning of each action. There was no hint of emotion in his voice. No histrionics. Yet, as his discourse progressed, I watched as the man sitting beside me bowed his head into his open hands and, overwhelmed, began to weep. Another man directly behind me shrieked the Name of God - "*Allah!*" - in ecstasy. In front of me another fainted dead away. I looked around me and the entire assembly was overcome, weeping unashamedly, shaking their heads at the power of the knowledge quietly articulated by this austere man of God.

He was one of the greatest living interpreters of Sufism in Morocco, whose commentaries and *qasa'id* were subtle, powerful and ecstatic, yet he personified sobriety on the Path. His discourses were delivered with scholarly gravitas but induced ecstasy and awe in his listeners. He lived a life without a trace of pretense. He was the proprietor of a small bolt-hole shop that sold household items near Bab Boujloud in Fes and, when he wasn't engaged in teaching or spiritual practice he could be found standing in front of his shop, like any other small trader. He had a pleasant, unpretentious house behind the Bab Boujloud Mosque where he delivered the Friday sermon. He was a family man who lived a sober, self-effacing life. He was, by all appearances and notwithstanding his ecstasy-inducing discourses, a restrained, conservative man of learning. But, of course, appearances can be misleading.

When Shaykh Mohamed ibn Al-Habib died in 1971 all his disciples turned to Si Fudul for guidance. The Shaykh had appointed Si Fudul as his *Khalifa* before he died and there were many who assumed he would inherit the Shaykh's mantle. Yet Si Fudul re-

92

fused, even though he would have been accepted by acclamation. The great Saharan saint Sidi Mohammed Bil Kurshi had also refused the role, leaving a vacuum that was not filled for decades.

It is hard for an outsider to understand how deeply troubling the loss of a living Shaykh is for the disciple and there is a natural human tendency to fill the immense gap left by the death of one's guide with a comforting placeholder. Many Sufi orders become hereditary in this way, with the son of the shaykh taking the mantle by acclamation to sustain the way. The great *awliya* within the Darqawiyya-Habibiyya Order had the profound integrity not to settle for what might have been reassuring and the Habibiyya carried on for decades, surviving on the extraordinarily powerful practice and legacy of the great 20th century shaykh. During this period, numerous people tried to declare themselves as Shaykh of the Order, but Si Fudul and others quashed these false claims.

One of my teachers in Makkah Al-Mukarramah, Shaykh Ismail, once said to me, "There is nothing worse on the face of the earth than the man of false claims." The living Shaykh is the spiritual equivalent of a heart or neurosurgeon, with the power to heal hearts and minds. An unqualified pretender without the authentic transmission, knowledge and authority from God and His Prophet, peace and blessings be upon him, can be as lethal and dangerous as a medical quack and can do untold damage to the unwitting or misguided soul.

Moulay Al-Arabi Ad-Darqawi wrote:

"Beware, beware lest you allow yourself to be deceived by someone, for how many there are who appear to be preaching for God when in reality they are only preaching for their desires."

Shaykh Ismail also told me succinctly, "Anyone who claims to be a Shaykh of *ma'rifa* is a liar." The true Shaykh doesn't have to make a claim. He simply is. It doesn't mean that the true Shaykh doesn't acknowledge his role. He simply doesn't have to stand up and proclaim and defend his claims. One pretender to the mantle of Ibn Al-Habib created a great deal of confusion when he made his claim, which reached as far away as Makkah Al Mukarramah, where I was living. Si Fudul knew the man and I had been asked by someone living in Makkah to ask Si Fudul his opinion on the matter. I posed the question. With a withering look, Si Fudul shook his head and said dismissively, "He behaves with the hauteur of a king. This is not the behavior of a true shaykh. This fellow only ever had authority to call people to Islam, nothing more."

At that point in my life I was without a living shaykh and was deeply concerned about this as all the great Sufi treatises stress the importance of keeping company with a living master. I asked Si Fudul what to do and he said, "In this time it is very difficult to find a living shaykh, nearly impossible. Make the sacred law (*Shariah*) your shaykh."

By the Grace of God, I did find a living shaykh, and eventually a living shaykh for the Habibiyya emerged, recognized by Si Fudul before he passed away. In this interim period I tried to follow the advice of this great, illuminated scholar. May God be well pleased with him and cover him with Mercy and Grace and flood his grave with light until the Day of Rising.

"The lights of sages precede their words, so that wherever illumination occurs, there the expression arrives."

Ibn Ata'illah Al-Iskandari*

---

* *Al-Hikam*, translated by Victor Danner.

TWENTY-FOUR HOURS

He lived in the Sahara beyond the Atlas Mountains in the oasis settlement of Touroug, a mud-brick *ksar*, built in the ancient style, a honeycomb of dwellings interlinked by passageways. He was considered one of the greatest saints of Morocco. His name inspired awe and reverence.

In his youth he had been a *majdhoub*, a holy madman, whose intoxication (*jadhb*) was so powerful that he could not live in ordinary society. Some men never emerge from this condition and can never function in polite society. They are technically mad but spiritually quite sane. When the great Sufi Shibli was accused of being mad, he retorted, "In your eyes I am mad and you are sane. May God increase me in my madness and increase you in your sanity!" It takes a great master with knowledge of both the outward and hidden sciences to be able to bring the *majdhoub* back to the ordinary world while preserving and enhancing his spiritual attainment. Sidi Mohamed Bil Kurshi came under the care and guidance of Shaykh Mohamed ibn Al-Habib, who restored his equilibrium and elevated his state.

When Imam Shadhili was asked why he did not write books, he answered, "My companions are my books." In this sense, Sidi Mohamed Bil Kurshi had been "written" by his Shaykh.

He was believed to be the spiritual heir of Shaykh Mohamed

95

ibn Al-Habib and when the Shaykh died in 1972 it was assumed that Sidi Mohamed Bil Kurshi would succeed him to lead the order. When he was called on to take the mantle of Mohamed ibn Al-Habib, he rejected the overtures, saying, "I am not a shaykh! I am not anything!"

Although he had re-entered the world and was the master of his immediate community, he remained reclusive, rarely venturing out beyond his desert home, which became a nexus of spirituality. Those who had been able to make the journey always returned in a state of awe.

In consequence, Touroug took on a mystical significance and became a place of pilgrimage, an audience with its master the goal for many seekers. At the time, it took the better part of two days to get to Touroug from Northern Morocco. You had to negotiate the Atlas Mountains and cross the Tafilalet to reach the remote *ksar*. It was a grueling journey. Yet, once you arrived, you were on a twenty-four hour time-clock. No outsider was permitted to stay in Touroug for more than one day. Twenty-four hours and you were politely but firmly sent packing. No one seemed to question this rigid protocol but it seemed somehow unreasonable to me. Why not the traditional three days?

One of the most common remarks one heard was the near invisibility of the saint. One visitor came for the first time with a group of *fuqara* who had met the great man before. They sat in the long reception, drinking tea, performing *dhikr* and awaiting the appearance of the *wali*. Finally the novice turned to one of his companions and asked, "When are we going to meet the *wali*?" His companion answered, "He's the one that has been serving you tea for the last hour."

In 1981 I was finally able to make the arduous journey over the Atlas Mountains and into the Tafilalet on the edge of the Northern Sahara to meet the legendary *wali'ullah*. We arrived in Touroug before sunset. From a distance, the *ksar* emerged on the horizon like a burnished mythical apparition. It was camouflaged at first, looking like a mound of earth ringed by palms and white desert. As we came close we could see the irregular outlines of the mud brick settlement. Entering into this small oasis was not so much like moving into another time as of moving out of time and space altogether. We were guided in to the *ksar* through a disorienting labyrinth of steps and passageways which brought to mind the optical illusions in M.C. Escher's hallucinatory lithographs. We were led to a long room with raised wood-frame cushioned sofas around the walls.

This turned out to be the home of Sidi Mohamed Bil Kurshi. We were each handed a woven palm whisk to keep away vicious biting desert flies which buzzed around the room until sunset, at which time they swarmed into the desert night, clustering around the date palms. We sang *qasa'id* from the Diwan of Ibn Al-Habib as tea was prepared.

This was the most peaceful place I had ever been. The walls were permeated with remembrance of God. The people were marinated in remembrance of God. Within minutes, without doing anything, we were floating on a sea of tranquility. I had never been so swiftly transported into such a peaceful state so effortlessly.

Moulay Al-'Arabi Ad-Darqawi, may God be well pleased with him, would say to his disciples, "Relax the mind and learn to swim." It was there in Touroug that I first understood this saying. My mind relaxed. Thoughts evaporated. My heart was afloat. I was swimming! This was way beyond good vibes. I hesitate to say this, but we were completely stoned on the atmosphere; it was enthralling, addictive. Within less than 10 minutes I never wanted to leave this place. I felt as if this was how life should always be.

As we sat in this blissful state, singing *qasa'id*, men passed in and out of the room. Unlike my predecessor I recognized Sidi Mohamed Bil Kurshi as soon as he entered. His face was beautiful, smooth, leonine and illuminated. He was wreathed in a white beard. He wore the green Darqawi turban. His presence was numinous and light, like a breath. He sat with us and tended to us. The atmosphere in his presence was at once unreal and completely natural.

Braziers were brought inside the long room and skewers of meat were cooked right in front of us. Sidi Mohamed Bil Kurshi turned the skewers himself. We ate the meat with bread and used our fly whisks to clear the smoky air. Before retiring we were shown to the lavatories. One would have expected they would have been primitive and malodorous. On the contrary, these waterless latrines had a rich, perfumed smell. Waste was covered by dried camel dung which smelled like new mown grass. We then stretched out on the divans and slept until dawn.

At dawn we were led by candlelight through the dark passageways to the mosque at the center of the *ksar*. The narrow passageways were open to a sliver of night sky flanked by high walls. One could see stars above. This was a primordial environment. There was no trace of modernity. We prayed the dawn prayer behind the imam and recited the *wird* in the half light. When the *wird* was completed we were led back to the home of the saint through the narrow passageways under the cold coppery sky.

After breakfast we were asked to make the obligatory trip to register with the local district police authority. In the midst of this intoxicating encounter I resisted, but to protect the community had to leave the *ksar* and show face. Compared to the ethereal gathering we had left, the police outpost seemed vile, squalid and degenerate. Bottles of Moroccan wine were standing in one corner of the commandant's office. Official formalities done, we rushed back to the blessed company of our host where the remembrance of God was the only intoxicant.

His son took me on a walk outside the *ksar* to show me the place they held their *Eid* prayers in the white desert. Nearby was a graveyard, each grave marked by a pot filled with stones. The desert custom was for every member of the community to invoke God thousands of times, marking their invocation with stones from the surrounding desert. These stones would fill the pot that served as a gravestone for the deceased. The surroundings were bleak and yet strangely arresting. He spoke of the pull of the world, which seduced many of the younger men to the cities. We tend to romanticize what we don't have. Surrounded by the desert with the *ksar* in the background I reflected on the transience of life. Everything was passing away. I was passing away. This unearthly community living in a city of sand and mud was passing away. I had an overpowering sense of evanescence.

I had been asked by someone from Makkah to ask Sidi Mohamed Bil Kurshi an awkward question about a person he knew who had gone astray. By the end of our stay in Touroug this was the last thing I wanted to do but I had promised to pose the question and, against my better judgment, I did. As soon as the words came out of my mouth I knew I'd made a mistake. Sidi Mohamed Bil Kurshi's sharp response was, "I don't know and you shouldn't think about it!" It was a rebuke delivered with lightning speed but with graceful indifference, more admonition than blame. He was giving me a lesson in good thoughts (*husnu al-dhann*). Once he had left the room, my companion Sidi Ali slapped his forehead, shook his head, chuckled and said, "If I'd known you were going to ask that question, I wouldn't have come along."

Sidi Ali once told my friend and spiritual brother Shakir Massoud-Priest, "It's like you're travelling in the desert. You're hot and thirsty and on the horizon you see a green line and you know there is water there but as you come closer you start looking at the details. You see someone beating his donkey. You see something else that's ugly. You need to step back and hold on to your original perception, which is the green and water, and not get too involved in the details. This is *husnu al-dhann*."

Sidi Mohamed Bil Kurshi walked out with us to see us off and say his farewells. At the door I turned to him and apologized for asking my awkward question. He smiled kindly, as if to say, "It's okay, just don't do it again," and then he closed his eyes and made a long supplication for me.

As we drove along the desert tracks in the fading winter light, with the taupe colored mud *ksar* receding in the distance I suddenly grasped why we only had twenty-four hours. Without this rigid time perimeter everybody would have converged on this fragile community. Every seeker would want to settle in and stay forever. The life here was spiritual perfection.

Sidi Mohamed Bil Kurshi passed away on 29 August 2012 (11 Shawwal 1433 A.H.) at the age of 110. May God be well pleased with him.

**"O how long shall we,
like children in the earthly sphere
Fill our lap with dust and stones and shards?
Let us give up the earth and fly heavenwards,
Let us flee from childhood to the banquet of men.
Behold how the earthly frame has entrapped thee!
Rend the sack and raise thy head clear."**

Maulana Jalalud'din Rumi*

---

*   From the *Diwan*, translated by William C. Chittick.

THE CENTENARIAN

By the time we met him, he was well over 100 years of age and had lost his sight. He had for eight decades devoted his life to the acquisition of knowledge and blessing. He was the great grandson of the 19th century Sufi master Sidi Al 'Arabi Al-Hawari and had been initiated by 52 of the greatest Sufi masters of the 19th and 20th centuries, including the famed Algerian Shaykh Ahmed Mustafa Al-'Alawi. His name was Sidi Mohamed Al-Sahrawi but we always referred to him as the *Wali* of Bahlil, after the small village he lived in outside Fes. According to Shaykh Moulay Hashem Balghiti, he had a great sense of humor but I remember him for his gravitas and his ardent love of God.

He made one of the most incisive statements on the human condition I have ever heard. It was this:

"The sickness of the human heart is, 'what shall I do?'"

This sums up our spiritual malaise. We don't know what to do. Spirituality is the science of what to do. The Messenger of God, may God bless him and give him peace, said, "The religion is action" (*al-deenu mu'aamalah*); when we don't know what to do, when we are in doubt, we become heart-sick.

One member of our group had been struggling on the Path. He asked the saint, "What do you do if you perform remembrance of God for year after year but it never reaches the heart?"

He replied, "You keep on invoking God because you never know when your invocation will take hold of the heart. Sometimes the effects of remembrance cannot be felt until the moment before you die. Have patience. Persist. Never give up."

Although he had been initiated by Shaykh Al-'Alawi, he was adamantly opposed to his practice of putting his disciples into spiritual retreat (*khalwa*). He recalled that he knew two brilliant young Algerian scholars Shaykh Al-Alawi had placed in *khalwa*. They emerged from the retreat insane. "They are still insane," he remarked.

Years later a member of our group disregarded this admonition, entering into an 'Alawiyya *khalwa* - and lost his mind.

In the aftermath of the death of Shaykh Mohamed ibn Al-Habib, the *fuqara* awaited the acclamation of his successor. For years no one emerged. There were many great saints of the Habibiyya Order at that time but none of these men admitted to the spiritual authority to guide the *fuqara*, although some lesser men laid claim to the role and were rebuked. Among the *fuqara* there was one younger man, an elegant and prosperous businessman named Moulay Hashem Balghiti. His father had been a great Sufi saint but, at the time Moulay Hashem seemed to be no more than a successful young businessman and sincere disciple. During one of our meetings with Sidi Mohamed Al-Sahrawi he said, almost as an afterthought, "You know, Moulay Hashem is a *wali'ullah.*" This seemed a strange remark at the time because the young man bore no obvious signs of sainthood beyond being a man of obvious piety and a generous host. A quarter century later, he emerged as the successor to Ibn Al-Habib, confirmed by all the living saints, and revived this moribund Sufi Order.

I visited Sidi Mohamed Al-Sahrawi in 1981 at his home in Bahlil. He had the largest set of prayer beads (*tasbih*) I had ever seen hanging on the wall of his *minzah*. When one from our group commented on this gargantuan rosary, he chuckled and said that he'd been offered an enormous sum of money to sell the prayer beads but refused. We sat and invoked God. He was almost childlike in his love of invocation. He wept when we sang from the *Diwan* of Ibn Al-Habib and threw himself into an impromptu *hadra*.

I asked him how to perfect my circumambulation (*tawaf*) of the Kaaba. He told me that I should make sure to kiss the Black Stone at least once during the seven circuits; that this was like kissing the Hand of God.

Sidi Mohamed Al-Sahrawi took me close to him, put his arm around me. He took his gigantic *tasbih* off the hook on his wall and placed it around my neck. He confessed to me, "I only want to have a good opinion of people. I only want to think good thoughts." May God bless him and cover him with Mercy.

**"Do not abandon the Invocation
because you do not feel
the Presence of God therein.
For your forgetfulness of the Invocation of Him
is worse than your forgetfulness
in the Invocation of Him.
Perhaps He will take you from an Invocation
with forgetfulness to one with vigilance,
and from one with vigilance to one
with the Presence of God,
and from one with the Presence of God to one
wherein everything but the Invoked is absent."**

Ibn Ata'illah Al-Iskandari*

* *Al-Hikam*, translated by Victor Danner.

TRANSMISSION

Sayyid Abu Bakr Attas Al-Habshy lived close to my home, in a simple house on a basalt hillside in the Nuzha District of Makkah Al-Mukarramah, but without accompanying my shaykh Sayyid Omar Abdullah I would never have met him. One of the greatest living saints of Makkah, a man of austerity, sobriety and profound knowledge, he was a recluse who never left his house except to attend the Friday congregational prayers. Sayyid Omar and I would visit Sayyid Attas after the Friday prayer and would sit with him until the afternoon prayer. He and Sayyid Omar had known each other for many years and would hold spiritual conversation while I looked on and listened. Visiting Sayyid Attas would become a Friday ritual whenever Sayyid Omar was in Makkah.

On one of these visits I brought my friend, an heir to an oil fortune who had embraced Islam several years earlier. He had spent a lot of time in Saudi Arabia but had never had contact with people of the Path.

When we entered, Sayyid Attas was already sitting with a seeker from Indonesia who was asking him to transmit the *Talqin* to him. *Talqin* is the direct oral transmission of the *Shahada*, the Muslim profession of faith – "I witness that there is no god but God and I witness that Mohamed is the Messenger of God" (*ash-hadu an la ilaha illa llah wa ash-hadu anna Mohamedan Rasulullah*) – from person to person tracing all the way back to the tongue of the Prophet Mohamed, peace and blessings be upon him. It is very rare to find anyone with this unbroken chain of transmission. The Indonesian was pleading with Sayyid Attas to receive *Talqin*. At first Sayyid Attas was reluctant. He said he didn't feel ready to transmit the *Talqin*. The Indonesian persisted, swearing that he had travelled all the way from Indonesia specifically to receive *Talqin* from Sayyid Attas. Finally, Sayyid Attas relented. When this happened, Sayyid Omar gripped my leg and whispered urgently, "You must repeat exactly what he says! This is very important." Sayyid Attas transmitted *Talqin* to our small group, intoning the first part of the *Shahadah* slowly and we repeated the formula. He then intoned the second part and we followed.

That was it. I had never seen Sayyid Omar as intensely engaged in anything as with this ritual. When we left the house of Sayyid Attas I asked Sayyid Omar why *Talqin* was so important. He said, "It makes the *Shahadah* easy on the tongue at the moment of death."

A few years later my friend passed away and it is my hope that this unexpected gift from Sayyid Attas eased his passing. May God have mercy on him and be well pleased with Sayyid Attas Al-Habshy.

I received *Talqin* on one other occasion, this time from the lips of my Shaykh Habib Ahmad Mashhur Al-Haddad. I was sitting in a small gathering of disciples at his home in Bani Malik in Jeddah. Suddenly, out of the blue, Al-Haddad transmitted the *Talqin* to our group with the same simplicity. May God accept our affirmation and forgive us for our wrong actions.

"Oh Lord of Majesty and Gifts, make us die on the religion of Islam."

A supplication*

---

* From Al Ratib Al Shahr, the litany of the *Saadatu l'Alawiyya*.

THE CURE

The Tijani *zawiya* of Shaykh Mohamed Al-Hafez Al-Tijani in Cairo attracted thousands of devotees year round who came to sit at the feet of this great scholar and spiritual master. Students, visitors and Tijani *fuqara* from across Africa, the Arab world, Southeast Asia and even from Europe came to meet him. By the time I met the Shaykh in 1976 he was very advanced in years and completely blind but continued to meet his many visitors and offer teaching and counsel to all.

In his time, he and the other shaykhs of his order, had the greatest following of any Sufi *tariqa* on earth. Their disciples around the world numbered in the tens of millions. The Tijaniyya Sufi Order is one of the largest Sufi orders in Africa, founded by the 18th century Shaykh Sidi Abbas Ahmad ibn Mohamed Al-Tijani Al-Hassani, who is buried in the city of Fes in Morocco.

Shaykh Mohamed Al-Hafez was, as his name suggests, *hafiz* of (one who has completely memorized) Qur'an and considered one of the world's greatest living authorities on *hadith*, the traditions of the Prophet Mohamed, peace be upon him. He had committed hundreds of volumes of *hadith*, commentary and poetry to memory. His memory was the stuff of legend. Thousands of books filled one wall of his *zawiya* from floor to ceiling. One could only reach the top shelves with a ladder. He remembered every word in most of the books in his library. Once, a student asked him about obscure references to truffles. The Shaykh directed the student to the bookshelf, giving the titles of the books with references to truffles and exactly where these volumes were located, on such and such a shelf so many volumes to the right, etc. When the volumes were located the Shaykh told the student on which page the reference was located and the exact line, reciting the sentences before and after the reference. The student followed his instructions and found all the references.

I witnessed this astonishing gift at first hand. One afternoon I was sitting in the Shaykh's company with an Italian disciple who was attempting to translate an obscure poem by Shaykh Al-Akbar Muhyid'din Ibn Al-Arabi into Italian. He had a French translation of the poem but the published Arabic version he had seemed to be missing a stanza. He asked his Shaykh if he knew of the poem. The Shaykh instructed him to read the stanza before and the stanza after the missing verse. He did so. On hearing the two verses Shaykh Al-Tijani immediately and effortlessly dictated the missing verse to the disciple.

I first met Shaykh Mohamed Al-Hafez at his *zawiya* in Cairo during Ramadan. I had accompanied a group of friends who were all studying at the *Madinat Al-Buhooth Al-Islami*, which was a school established to prepare foreign students for higher studies at Al-Azhar University. We visited the Shaykh at fast breaking and remained through the night prayer and prayed the *tarawih* behind him. When the *tarawih* prayers were completed we came forward as a group to greet the Shaykh. He shook our hands as we were briefly introduced by name and he welcomed us all. Then he retired to his apartments. That was that.

I had only recently settled in Egypt and was having enormous trouble adjusting. I had been accustomed to the rarified company of Sufis and the relatively pristine romantic ambience of Moroccan Sufi Islam. Suddenly I was thrown into the rough chaos of Cairo, with its crowds, cacophony, craziness and reeking streets. I attended night classes at *Madinat Al-Bohooth Al-Islami,* in which the exhausted teacher – on his third job for the day - would put up an exercise on the chalkboard and then fall fast asleep at his desk.

During the days I taught English literature at what was then Egypt's premiere private school. To get there I would have to take the horrifically crowded Bab Al-Luk train from Sakinat station near my flat to Bab Al-Luk Station in the center of town and then take a bus from Tahrir Square to the school in Zamalek. Young men wouldn't wait for the train to stop on the platform but would leap through open windows to get a seat. Surrealistic fist fights broke out in the over-packed train on a daily basis. In the mornings and evenings people would hang off the sides of the train and clamber up on top for a treacherous free ride. I witnessed many accidents and several fatalities during this time. On one occasion a young man was hit head-on by the train and his body flew past my window. The man sitting beside the window next to me saw the mutilated flying corpse and blanched in horror. Then he turned to me with a resigned shrug. *"Ma'alesh,"* he said. "Oh well."

I finally snapped one day when a sweating middle-aged fat man elbowed past a young woman who was ascending the steps to the bus in front of me, crushing her against the door and nearly pushing her off into the street, just to get a seat. Outraged, I approached him and told him his behavior was the same as an animal's. (I didn't think he understood English.) He grabbed my arm. *"I weell keell you!"* he hissed, squeezing the button off my shirt cuff. The other passengers separated us – they had seen what he had done to the young woman. The bus driver apologized profusely and refused to take a fare from me. The passengers were very kind, but I had reached the end of my tether. The city was grinding me down.

The daily struggle of surviving the public transport system, the begging, the stench of uncollected garbage and deteriorated infrastructure finally got to me. As a spoiled American I was simply not ready for all the anarchy and pandemonium of Cairo. I went into deep culture shock. I started to hate Egypt and Egyptians.

Finally I became violently ill. I was convinced that my bad

thoughts had poisoned me and made me sick. I suffered for three days with a high fever and agonizing pains throughout my body. I confessed to my wife that I was certain this was from the really venomous thoughts that had overcome me.

On the third day, we received a knock on the door. It was Shaykh Al-Tijani's son Ahmed. He was about 30 years old. He had come all the way out to Sakanaat from Cairo by train. In those days the journey would have taken at least one hour each way, if not longer. He asked for me. I appeared at the door. He said, "My father has sent me to you. He said, 'Haroon is sick. You must go to him and give him this.'" Despite our fleeting group encounter a week earlier, we had never had any other exchange. I had no idea the blind Shaykh was even aware of my existence. I don't know how he knew that I was ill. His son handed me an envelope and immediately excused himself to make the long journey back to Cairo. When I opened the envelope I found it contained enough money to live on for a month. This sudden and unexpected act of generosity had a sublimely therapeutic affect on me. I had let bad thoughts overwhelm me and had conceived of a loathing for Egyptians. Yet here was an Egyptian that had suddenly, without warning, reached out to someone he didn't know with a simple, transcendent gift.

When I awoke the next morning, my illness disappeared, my health was restored and, most importantly, my heart was cured.

"They are the skilful physicians whom God has assisted with a spirit from Him, so that they treated the diseases of hearts with wisdom, and poured guidance into pleasant and permissible moulds in order to take the ordinary people along the road of their desires to the desired truth..."

Al-Habib Ahmad Mashhur Al-Haddad*

* Key to the Garden, translated by Mostafa Al-Badawi.

MAJESTY

His presence was majestic. His face was inexpressive. I never once saw him smile, although I'm sure he must have. He seldom betrayed emotions except when he made supplication to God. His extended supplications following a night of invocation drove his listeners to tears. His heartrending cry to the Lord of All Being for help and succor swept his audience along like a flood tide. Devotees would converge on gatherings just to hear his supplications seal an evening.

Habib Abdul Qadir Al-Saqqaf would often attend gatherings with my shaykh Habib Ahmed Mashhur Al-Haddad, his spiritual brother. Together they seemed to form a delicate balance. Al-Saqqaf embodied Majesty (*Al-Jalal*) while Al-Haddad embodied Beauty (*Al-Jamal*). Gatherings with these men were suffused with blessing.

He was a spiritual lord who commanded enormous influence in the Kingdom of Saudi Arabia against all odds, for Sufism was banned and supressed by the religious authorities and Al-Saqqaf was one of the world's preeminent Sufi masters.

One day my shaykh Sayyid Omar Abdullah returned from a visit to Al-Saqqaf at his home in Jeddah. His visit had produced an unveiling. "I realized," he said with grave certainty, "that Al-Saqqaf has reached the station of *baqa* (subsistence in God). He has been completed." Sayyid Omar rarely discussed the spiritual stations of his peers. The supreme stations of knowledge (*ma'ri-*

fa) on the Sufi path are *fana* and *baqa*, referred to in Sura Rahman (55:26-27):

"All that is on the earth shall pass away (*faan*)
And the Face of your Lord will abide forever (*yabqa*),
full of Majesty and Generosity."

The twin doctrines of *fana* and *baqa* were first articulated by the 9th century Baghdadi saint Abu Sa'id Al-Kharraz who wrote, "*Fana* is annihilation of consciousness of *'ubudiyyat*, (human individuality as a servant of the Lord) and *baqa* is subsistence in the contemplation of *ilahiyyat* (divinity). According to 'Ali bin Uthman Al Hujwiri in *Kashf Al Mahjub*, this means that "it is an imperfection to be conscious in one's actions that one is a man, and one attains real manhood when one is not conscious of them, but is annihilated so as to not see them, and becomes subsistent through beholding the action of Allah... Abú Ya'qúb Nahrajúrí says: 'A man's true *'ubúdiyyat* (servitude) lies in *fana* and *baqa'*...'"*

To an ordinary person these exalted stations are incomprehensible. Yet, through observation, through subtle indications, one might sense the marks of attainment.

At one point I had reached a crisis regarding my residency in Saudi Arabia. I tried to solve the problem through ordinary channels but without success. I had reached a bureaucratic impasse. I mentioned this to Sayyid Omar and he immediately suggested that we refer this problem to Al-Saqqaf. The idea of approaching this great saint with something as trivial and mundane as my residency problem seemed completely inappropriate but my teacher insisted and he was far wiser than I. In the event it afforded me a glimpse of Habib Abdul Qadir in action.

Al-Saqqaf was the preeminent Sufi in the Kingdom of Saudi Arabia and many of the country's wealthiest and most influential citizens were numbered among his thousands of disciples,

* *Kashf Al Mahjub*, translated by Reynold Nicholson

112

including the general in charge of the immigration authority. So one morning we drove from my home in Makkah to Al-Saqqaf's large home in Jeddah. On the road between Makkah and Jeddah, Sayyid Omar spoke of Al-Saqqaf's dramatic rise to the position of spiritual authority he enjoyed in Saudi Arabia in spite of the fact that the practice of Sufism (*Tasawwuf*) was suppressed by the Kingdom's religious authorities. Behind the affluence and influence he enjoyed was a quarter century of abasement and service on the Path in Hadramaut where he reached an exalted spiritual station. With the Communist takeover of South Yemen, he was forced into exile in the Western Province of the Kingdom, where he was greeted as a spiritual master.

When we arrived at the Shaykh's home he was already seated in his *majlis*, attending to the individual needs of a procession of students, disciples and petitioners. Sayyid Omar brought me near to Al-Saqqaf and I was able to observe his audiences at close range. One wealthy merchant came to the Shaykh with a large sum of money, bundled in stacks of high denomination notes wrapped in clear plastic. I watched with fascination as the disciple handed over what must have amounted to a hundred thousand Saudi riyals to Al-Saqqaf. Habib Abdul Qadir took the package without a change of expression, invoked a blessing on the merchant and without looking at the package casually tossed it over his shoulder and turned to his next visitor. The whole transaction didn't last more than about one minute.

Although we were sitting beside the Shaykh, each transaction was carried out with a great sense of intimacy between disciple and master with most conversations inaudible. Men came with questions, problems and simply for the blessing. After some time had passed a young man approached the Shaykh, clearly in distress. We watched as he explained his need. Habib Abdul Qadir called upon one of his assistants and directed him to bring the package of cash he had tossed aside a half hour earlier. The assistant handed the package to Al-Saqqaf who passed it on to the young man. He had never even looked at the contents. He was like a spiritual filter through which the world flowed.

When our time came, Sayyid Omar greeted his old friend and explained my predicament. Al-Saqqaf took out a phone contact book, thumbed through it and reached for the phone sitting on the floor beside him. He dialed a number from the book. When the party on the other end answered he said brusquely without any introduction, "Yusuf, Sayyid Omar and Haroon are coming to you. See to their needs," and hung up. He had just delivered a blunt order to a high-ranking Saudi general. He sent us off to the Passport Office. The General saw us and solved my problem on the spot.

The last time I saw Al-Saqqaf was at the memorial for my beloved Shaykh Habib Ahmed Mashhur Al-Haddad, held in an empty lot covered with carpets outside the Al-Haddad family home in Bani Malek. He was, by this time, seriously ill and had to be carried to the gathering. With the passing of Al-Haddad and the infirmity of Al-Saqqaf the world seemed an infinitely more precarious place.

May God protect us from the turmoil and temptations of this world and bring us near to His Friends in the next.

Habib Abdul Qadir Al Saqqaf passed away in 2010 (1431AH) at the age of 100, may God be pleased with him.

"He whom God has illuminated sees Him in all things."

Muhyid'din Ibn Al 'Arabi*

---

* *Futuhat Al-Makkiyah* (Makkan Revelations) cited in Voyage of No Return by Claude Addas.

RIVER OF HEAVEN

When I first sat in his company he was living in a large room in the Al-Azhar Mosque complex in Cairo. He had been the Imam of the Holy Mosque in Makkah Al-Mukarramah and was among the favorite scholars of His Majesty King Faisal of Saudi Arabia, who would invariably sit in his company when he visited the Holy Mosque. In his later years he retired to Egypt from Saudi Arabia and became an Imam of Al-Azhar Mosque from where he would give discourse and oversee circles of remembrance twice weekly, on Sundays and Thursdays. On these evenings, every visitor was fed. During the month of Ramadan he would preside over a fast-breaking meal every evening open to all. Hundreds attended. Many were visibly very poor.

Shaykh Saleh Al-Ja'fari was an orator of immense power, a great Sufi scholar in a world that had largely turned its back on Sufism. He would sit majestically erect upon a raised platform and begin to speak to whoever gathered in his presence. His discourse was so compelling that hundreds would assemble to hear him. His speech was like a wide, slow-flowing river, like the Nile, a river of heaven. His voice was resonant and forceful, his knowledge deep and broad. He had written hundreds of odes (*qasa'id*) on the Way. His talks were vibrant and animated and one could be forgiven for mistaking the power of discourse for physical power. He was, in fact, very frail and had to be supported to and from his seat in Al-Azhar Mosque.

He did not countenance pietism. Once a member of his audience asked him a pretentious religious question about whether or not it was permissible to look at women, to which he responded in his booming voice, "Don't ask me this question! You already know the answer. I will give you more useful advice. Next time you're sitting in a *qahwa* (traditional Arab café) smoking *shisha* (hubbly bubbly, *nargilah* or water pipe) and a young girl passes by and you undress her with your eyes – and you will without any doubt do that - just say, *"Astaghfirullah!"* (I ask forgiveness of God)."

On another occasion during his discourse, a member of the audience cried out the Name of God, *"Allah!"*, as if he was awestruck, whenever the Shaykh said anything profound. After several ejaculations from the listener, Shaykh Saleh stopped his discourse and said, "Tell this man to be quiet. Stop crying out like this!"

During the 1970s there was a modest revival of interest in Sufism in Egypt. Two of Egypt's most influential scholars were Sufis, the Shaykh of Al-Azhar, Dr. Abdul Halim Mahmoud, and the Arab world's most popular orator, Shaykh Metwally Sha'rawi, who was a disciple of the great Algerian Sufi Shaykh Mohamed Bil Qaid. There was an emerging fascination in the mystical aspects of the Path, which included the hidden spiritual hierarchy of saints that had been described in classical Sufi literature. Many Sufi orders were claiming that their shaykh was the *"Qutb"* or Pole of the Universe, a reality which is, in this wayward age, irrelevant to ordinary people. One afternoon my wife and I attended one of Shaykh Saleh's discourses in Al-Azhar. He spoke about the *Qutb*, saying, "All these shaykhs are claiming to be *Qutb*! We know that there is only one *Qutb* at any time. What's going on? Are these men lying? No. They believe they're the *Qutb* because they have reached the *Maqam Al-Qutubiyya* – the Station of being *Qutb*. They have mistaken the station with the role. They are mistaken."

Shaykh Saleh explained that people today have come to believe that saints are infallible but this is not the case. Saints can make mistakes. Only the Prophets can be said to be infallible and this is because "they are disciplined by God."

Then Shaykh Saleh told a long complicated story about a *Qutb*. In the story the *Qutb* had to do many terrible things in order to preserve the harmony of the world, including seeing to the death of a child who was destined to become a murderous tyrant. At the end of this convoluted and awful tale, Shaykh Saleh said, "Why would anybody want to be a *Qutb*?" He shivered. "I don't want to be a *Qutb*!"

During that period, my wife's uncle, a gold merchant who had been a member of the Muslim Brotherhood and had spent years in prison during the time of Gamal Abdul Nasser, invited me repeatedly to visit his Sufi Shaykh. I wasn't interested in Egyptian politics and assumed that his shaykh was a Muslim Brotherhood shaykh with some Sufi connection. I never took him up on his invitation. I was a fool. His shaykh was the great Sufi master Shaykh Hassan Mawlatawi, who was, I learned many years later, the living *Qutb* of his age.

May God be well pleased with Shaykh Saleh Al-Ja'fari and Shaykh Hassan Mawlatawi and let us benefit from their blessing in spite of our many imperfections.

"Do not keep company with anyone whose state does not inspire you and whose speech does not lead you to God."

Shaykh Ibn Ata'illah Al-Iskandari*

* *Al-Hikam*, translated by Victor Danner.

117

THREE HUNDRED

In London he came to visit with an official entourage, but when he sat within our circle he assumed his essential role as spiritual guide. He spoke of Sahl ibn Abdullah Al-Tustari, may God be well pleased with him, who, as a youth, was instructed by his shaykh to pray constantly and prostrate much until one day his heart stayed in prostration even after his body rose up. He had reached the Station of Prostration (*Maqam Al-Sujud*) and his heart remained prostrate for the rest of his life. He told this story in a state of serene rapture, as if he himself subsisted in the station he described, but God knows best. His presence both electrified and calmed the assembly. His rapture was infectious... and unforgettable.

This was in 1975 when Dr. Abdul Halim Mahmoud was Shaykh Al-Azhar, the single most important official religious figure in Sunni Islam at a time of dramatic change for the Muslim world. The sudden wealth flowing into the Muslim states from the OPEC price rises had given the Islamic world new political and economic clout and a place on the world stage. King Faisal's pan-Islamic movement had revived an interest in institutional Islam as an alternative to Arab Nationalism which was in decline in the aftermath of the Fall of Jerusalem in 1967. The October War of 1973 had placed Egypt back at the political center and given Anwar Sadat new prestige as a strong Arab leader.

Sorbonne educated, Dr. Abdul Halim was the most cosmopolitan religious figure in Egypt with a finely tuned political acuity. He was also a Sufi scholar with deep spiritual roots and a prolific writer on Sufism. And, most importantly, he was one of God's saints with a secret group of disciples. He would only accept a disciple who had first seen him in a dream and it is said that since his death he continues to teach his disciples in dreams and visions.

When I settled in Egypt in 1976 it was Shaykh Al-Azhar who facilitated my stay and signed an official document that I had converted to Islam in his presence, even though I had been a practicing Muslim for years. He watched over those of us from the West who had embraced Islam and made sure that we kept good company.

The last time I saw him was in Los Angeles immediately after Anwar Sadat's historic trip to Israel, which had endeared the Egyptian leader to the West and branded him a traitor to the Arab and Islamic world. Shaykh Al-Azhar had been sent by Sadat to the US on an official visit to reach out to the Muslim community in America. He gave a talk at UCLA, where we went to meet him. We were able to sit with the Shaykh for a while and then moved with his entourage to the Central Mosque in Los Angeles. He led the prayers. I was thrilled to stand shoulder to shoulder and pray beside the legendary *qari* (reciter of Qur'an) Shaykh Mahmoud Khalil Al-Houssari. Shaykh Al-Azhar then gave a press conference. I remember the reporter from Newsweek asked, tongue in cheek, "Do you think that America could become a Muslim country?" Shaykh Al-Azhar answered with a twinkle in his eye, "Why not? Americans believe in God and Islam is the religion of God. It is not impossible." How things have changed.

Outside the mosque I met him. He greeted me warmly. I told him with some pride that three people had just converted to Islam with me. He smiled sweetly and said, "Why not three hundred?" His response left me deflated. Was he teaching me humility? Was he teaching me not to be satisfied with a small achievement but to aspire to greater things? I expected a pat on the back and felt that my efforts had been dismissed by this great man.

In retrospect, it occurred to me as I was setting down these memories decades later that one of the three souls who had converted to Islam was an intense and brilliant 18 year old former theological student who subsequently learned Arabic, traveled the world in search of knowledge, sitting with many of the great men of the Way and emerged as one of the most influential Muslim thinkers and orators in the West, reaching millions and guiding thousands on the path of Islam. He is known today as Shaykh Hamza Yusuf. In balance I would say he counts for three hundred, at the very least. Perhaps Shaykh Al-Azhar understood this with the eye of insight.

God knows best.

"Whoever wishes to see three hundred men in one man has only to look at me, for I have followed three hundred teachers and from each of them I have derived a quality..."

One of the men of the Path*

* From *Kitab nasab al-khirqa* by Esad Effendi, related in Quest for the Red Sulfur: The Life of Ibn 'Arabi by Claude Addas.

THE MERCHANT

One evening I walked into our *zawiya* in London and found my companions gathered around two elderly Sufis from Hadramaut who lived in Saudi Arabia. One was stout and one was thin. They sang *qasa'id* from great *awliya* of Hadramaut. Their voices were rough and unmusical but they sang with great passion and intensity and they transfigured the room.

I had just been married. My wife was from Makkah and we planned to live there. When I was introduced to these men and they were told that I was planning to resettle in Makkah, the stout one told me I could find them on Fridays in the Holy Mosque near Bab Al-Rahma.

When I finally arrived in Makkah I did try to find them near Bab Al-Rahma but in the vastness of the Holy Mosque I never did and eventually gave up looking. Their names slipped my mind and I forgot their faces.

A year or two after I arrived in Saudi Arabia I was with my shaykh Sayyid Omar Abdullah in Jeddah. One day he insisted that we visit a great Sufi, a wealthy trader, at his home in the Kandara District of Jeddah. He had been invited to lunch and he dragged me along. (Being dragged along by Sayyid Omar was one of my favorite pastimes.)

We parked outside a plain, large, undistinguished old stucco house, walked up the stairs to an apartment and came upon the trader, Shaykh Mohamed BaShaykh, reclining on a couch in the sitting room. As was his custom, he had returned from his office in the old souk, prayed the noon prayer and was resting until lunch was served. Every day guests would arrive – friends, family and visitors – and would have lunch with BaShaykh.

That first day, over the afternoon meal, Sayyid Omar introduced me. BaShaykh said casually, "I know Haroon. I met him in London." He had been the stout one. The thin man I came to learn was Shibli, who lived nearby. This was to be the first of many days I would sit at this great man's table.

Sayyid Omar had known BaShaykh for decades. They were old friends and companions on the Way. Sayyid Omar had enormous respect for him. Indeed, although not the richest, he was one of the most respected merchants in Jeddah. Sayyid Omar told me how he attained his wealth.

When he was a young man, like so many young men from Hadramaut, BaShaykh left his home to see the world and seek his fortune. He travelled to Mombasa and then to the island of Lamu, off the Swahili coast in Kenya. He was very poor and was sitting in the Riyadha Mosque, which had been built by the Hadrami *wali'ullah*, Habib Salih, the patron saint of Lamu.

As BaShaykh was leaving the mosque a man suddenly approached him and told him he must go to Jeddah where he would find his fortune. BaShaykh was headed elsewhere but when he arrived at the airstrip to leave the country he found that the flight he planned to take was cancelled and that, instead, there was a cargo plane on the tarmac ready to take off for Jeddah and was offered free passage to the Red Sea port. He climbed into the small aircraft and from that point the way became easy for him.

He made his fortune importing livestock from Sudan to Saudi Arabia for the pilgrims. He was very wealthy but he lived a life of simplicity and austerity. His greatest extravagance that I could see was the daily gathering he would hold in a large assembly room (*majlis*) he'd built on the ground floor of his house. Every evening dozens of Sufis would gather, remember God, and be fed.

Otherwise, he seemed utterly indifferent to his wealth. He carried out his business in a small, pokey office in the old *souk* in Jeddah and he slept on a cheap steel folding bed. I got the feeling that his sons chafed under their father's asceticism. He simply didn't care for anything the world had to offer. His knowledge was encyclopedic. His presence was medicinal.

The last time I saw BaShaykh was at the funeral of our Shaykh Habib Ahmed Mashhur Al Haddad. We greeted one another. The encounter was deeply poignant. Both my teachers had passed. BaShaykh was like a magnificent boulder on the shore soon to be covered by the inevitable rising tide.

"The true saint goes in and out amongst the people and eats and sleeps with them and buys and sells in the market and marries and takes part in social intercourse and never forgets God for a single moment."

Shaykh Abu Sa'id Fazlu'llah bin Abi'l Khair*

* From "The Secret of God's Mystical Oneness", translated by John O'Kane.

THE ENGLISH SAINT

The first authentic book on Sufism I had ever read was *A Muslim Saint of the 20th Century* (later re-titled *A Sufi Saint of the 20th Century*) on the life and teaching of the Algerian Shaykh Ahmad Mustafa Al-'Alawi. The author was Dr. Martin Lings, who at the time was Keeper of Oriental Manuscripts at the British Library. The book had a deep impact on me and was instrumental in sending me on the Sufi way. At around the same time I discovered a Folkways recording of a Yemeni Sufi *hadra* with annotations by Dr. Lings. I played the recording over and over again, longing to join this powerful celebration of remembrance.

So, in a very real sense, my journey began with Martin Lings, whose Muslim name was Abu Bakr Sirajud'din, and, although I only met him once, his presence and influence has, indirectly, been a guiding light for me through the course of my journey.

I once asked my shaykh Sayyid Omar Abdullah who among Western Sufis could have attained deep spiritual knowledge. Without hesitation and to my surprise he answered that it would be Martin Lings, who he had known since their days as students at the School of Oriental and African Studies in London. I asked him why and he said, "He has made the act of invocation the priority of his life and has organized his life around the remembrance, contemplation and worship of God."

The legacy of Martin Lings is unique and extraordinary. His writings on Sufism have guided generations of believers on the

Way and his sublime *Sira* (biography) on the Prophet, peace be upon him, is the finest in the English language. As a spiritual guide, he left a wonderfully useful system for keeping to the Path in the modern world. His disciples have had enormous influence on the literary and intellectual revival of Sufism in the West.

My meeting with Shaykh Abu Bakr was the result of a brief but moving friendship with his very first student. During my first sojourn in Egypt in 1976. I was introduced to Sidi Abdul Latif, a Swiss *faqir*, who had become an invalid after a freak accident. Although he was only in middle age, he was bedridden. He blamed his doctors, who had prescribed heavy doses of cortisone, which exacerbated his condition. He would say, "They have killed me, these doctors." While he was confined to his bed, he seemed otherwise relatively robust and I was sure his health would eventually be restored. Whenever he claimed to be dying, we tried to comfort him, saying, "No, you will be fine. God will heal you."

We would visit him at his home regularly and sing *qasa'id* from the *diwans*. He took great comfort in our visits. When we would arrive he would say without preamble, "Okay, let's start," and we would begin the invocation. During one period, I became very busy with work and study and didn't manage to visit Sidi Abdul Latif for a few weeks. Finally, I felt remiss and decided to pay him a visit. We climbed the stairs to his flat in the leafy suburb of Maadi. His young son Mohamed met us at the door, his face marked with grief. His father had passed away 8 days before. We were led to Sidi Abdul Latif's room. His wife was sitting in his bed, weeping and praying.

As Mohamed and his sister Rawhiya looked on, Sidi Abdul Latif's wife told us how he had died. He had asked for the Qur'an to be recited. He listened for a long time. Once the Qur'an had been recited he pointed his right index finger, repeated the Muslim confession *"ash-hadu an la ilaha illa 'llah wa ash-hadu anna Sayyidna Mohamedan Rasulullah"*. He looked to heaven and expired. The moment his spirit left his body, his visage, which dur ing his life had been strained with discomfort, became luminous and serene.

As I had spent considerable time with Sidi Abdul Latif before he died, Abdallah Schleifer, one of his close friends, asked me to write to Martin Lings, who was his guide, and describe my meetings with Sidi Abdul Latif. I did so and the letter was sent to him. Sometime later I received a message that Dr. Lings was moved by my letter and wanted to see me.

A few years' later I was passing through England and arranged to visit Dr. Lings at his home in Kent. At that time I was searching for a spiritual master and was intrigued by his writings and attracted to the Sufi order he led in England because many of my friends were members.

I took the train to the closest station to Shaykh Abu Bakr's home in Kent and was met on the platform by his wife Sayyida Rabia who drove me to their cottage on a leafy country road. The cottage had one of the most beautiful English gardens I have ever seen.

His presence was austere, serene and arid. He was, at once, profoundly English and yet profoundly oriental. He wore an immaculate Moroccan *djellaba* and *burnoose* and a perfectly wrapped white turban in his home. In my suit I felt entirely out of place and he draped another *burnoose* over my shoulders, which I wore for the duration of my visit. The atmosphere of his home was rarified and light. His voice was smooth and mellifluous; his speech slow and meticulous.

He thanked me for my letter and we spoke of Sidi Abdul Latif. We had a healthy lunch beautifully prepared by Sayyida Rabia. Over tea I told him that I was attracted to his order because many of my closest friends were initiates. He said, "That's not a very good reason." I shrugged and said, "Well that is the reason I have at the moment."

After tea we took a serene walk in Sidi Abu Bakr's exquisitely lush garden. I had a profound sense that our silent stroll around these paradisiacal grounds was steeped with meaning.

We said our farewells at the door and Sayyida Rabia drove me back to the station to catch my train back to London.

It was the last time I ever saw this great man, who was a treasure to mankind, a Muslim through and through and a true Man of God. May God be well pleased with him.

Martin Lings passed away on May 12 2005 at the age of 96.

Sufism is central, exalted, profound and mysterious; it is inexorable, exacting, powerful, dangerous, aloof ---- and necessary."

Martin Lings*

* From What is Sufism?.

GAZING AT THE HOUSE

I would meet him at dawn before the Kaaba in the *mataf* between the Station of Ismail and the Yemeni Corner where he would be sitting with his disciples invoking the Names of God and gazing at the House of God. While we were sitting in this way he said, "If you could see with the eye of insight you would see that the Kaaba is more than a building of stone; you would see its reality." We would pray the dawn prayer in congregation and then Shaykh Abdul Qadir 'Isa would lead us on the circumambulation (*tawaf*) around God's House. Normally, one makes a single *tawaf* of seven circuits. Shaykh Abdul Qadir would repeat the seven circuits of *tawaf* over and over and over again until sunrise.We would then all pray the sunrise prayer (*Salat Al-Shurouq*) and part ways. He did this every day he was in Makkah. I found this practice intoxicating…and taxing. Shaykh Abdul Qadir was always energized and exhilarated. He was consumed by the remembrance of God and enraptured by His House.

He was one of the most famous Sufis of his age, the successor to Shaykh Mohamed Al-Hashimi, who succeeded the Algerian Shaykh Ahmed Mustafa Al-'Alawi, may God be well pleased with them. I had heard about him when he was still residing in Aleppo and leading the 'Alawiyya Sufi Order in Syria. We knew of him through a Syrian disciple who was living and studying in England during the 1970s. He was the spiritual guide to tens of thousands of followers throughout Syria and abroad. His weekly gatherings in Aleppo were legendary, attracting thousands. During the 1980s, with the rise of the Muslim brotherhood and Islamic dissident groups, Sufis became suspect and Shaykh Abdul Qadir, as one of the most influential Sufis in Syria, was forced into exile. He first settled in Makkah Al Mukarramah as a guest of one of his disciples, a wealthy Saudi businessman.

When I arrived in Makkah in 1980 I was at a crossroads. I had been following the Sufi way for over 8 years and had been able to sit at the feet of many great men of the Path but I had never been under the direct discipline of a living shaykh of instruction. When I arrived in Makkah I had made it my intention to find a guide who could take me by the hand and keep me on the right path. So when I learned that Shaykh Abdul Qadir 'Isa was living in Makkah, I sought out his company.

The first thing he said to me when we were introduced was, "Haroon, you must have a living shaykh." During the time that I kept company with him he repeated this to me many times and yet, curiously, he never once encouraged me to take his hand. In their love for their Shaykh, his disciples pushed me to join their order but I could never bring myself to take this step. I half expected Shaykh Abdul Qadir to make some kind of overture but he never did. He was always kind to me and welcomed me into his circle but there was always a distance. Later on I came to learn that the relationship between the disciple (*murid*) and the shaykh is a grave matter, written in the unseen; that no authentic teaching shaykh can take on a disciple without the spiritual authority from God to do so. It is a matter of secrets. It is a matter of the heart.

However, Shaykh Abd Al-Qadir 'Isa was very clear in defining who an authentic teaching Shaykh actually is. He quoted from his own master, Shaykh Muhamed Al-Hashimi, who said:

"O my brother! Travel the path under the direction of a living Shaykh who knows Allah and is truthful and sincere; one who possesses correct knowledge, clear experiential taste, lofty spiritual will, and a well-pleasing spiritual state; a Shaykh who has travelled the path under the hands of true guides, having taken his manners from the possessors of manners; one who is well acquainted with the pathways; in order that he may save you from the pitfalls in your own spiritual journey and guide you to the state of being gathered (jama') with Allah."*

When a visitor mentioned someone who had recently claimed to be Sufi shaykh, Shaykh Abd Al-Qadir dismissed the pretender as a matter of fact, saying simply and with a shrug, "He who is connected to the one who is connected is connected and he who is connected to the one who is not connected is *not* connected."

His teaching revolved around the supererogatory (nawafil) practices. The pillars of Islam – prayer, fasting, the poor tax (zakat) and pilgrimage – were a given. The practice of Sufism is the application of the supererogatory. For most ordinary mortals, superogatory practices can be grueling. For Shaykh Abd Al-Qadir 'Isa the superogatory practices were like breathing air. His practice of the supererogatory was incessant, his devotion infectious. He would pray all the sunna prayers before and after each obligatory prayer. We would pray the tahajjud prayers in the depths of night. He never let up.

Most gatherings would culminate in a spiritual dance (hadra), which Shaykh Abdul Qadir would lead. Under his guidance the hadra was intense and bracing but very light. His singers had lilting angelic voices that soared above the rhythmic collective breath of the fuqara. But it was his practical advice that made the deepest impression on me.

I once asked Shaykh Abdul Qadir what the spiritual value of the lesser pilgrimage (umrah) was and he said quite simply, "Umrah burns up wrong actions." I had always loved umrah and was attached to its practice. This saying gave me even greater incentive to make the lesser pilgrimage because my wrong ac-

---

* From The Realities of Sufism, translated by Suraqah Abdul Aziz

tions were too numerous to count.

Another disciple mentioned that he had insomnia. Shaykh Abdul Qadir laughed and told him to rise and make supererogatory night prayers (*tahajjud*). He said, "The devil (*shaytan*) hates it when you pray and will make you drowsy and go to sleep. If not, you will have your reward."

He inspired intense devotion from his disciples. They loved him deeply. He was, on the surface, detached, brusque and sometimes brutally direct. Beneath the surface he was a sea of love and compassion.

I was blessed to have been able to spend time in his presence at a crossroads in my life. He kept me on the Path that eventually led me to a living master. May God be well pleased with him.

"My servant never ceases to draw near to Me through supererogatory works until I love him. Then, when I love him, I am his hearing through which he hears, his sight through which he sees, his hand through which he grasps, and his foot through which he walks."

Hadith Qudsi*

* *Sahih Al-Bukhari*

132

LOVE

"May God make me a feather in your wings"

Sidi Ahmed Al Badawi "Zwetan"*

* In a letter to his disciples, translated by Ezzad'ine Bettache

THE BELOVED

H e was among the greatest Sufi saints of the 20th century. It was said that he was one of the four spiritual Pillars (*Awtad*) in the hierarchy of saints, but God knows best. He was also the most humble man I have ever known. In the scheme of things, I was no one of importance, spiritually or temporally, yet when I would enter his presence he would struggle to his feet and stand in my honor on his game leg. He would call out my Muslim name with great love and reverence, "Haroooon, Haroon. *Allah, Allah, Allah!*", as if I was the most important man he had ever met.

I first met Habib Ahmed Mashhur bin Taha Al-Haddad shortly after settling in Saudi Arabia in 1980. A visitor from England who was staying with me in Makkah had heard about him and asked me to drive him to meet the Shaykh. I can't remember how we found the Al-Haddad family home, which was at that time in the old Kandara District of Jeddah, but we were welcomed warmly and spent many hours in his company. It was his humility, hospitality, kindness and natural forbearance that first struck me. Although he was already in his seventies he was full of life and had a beautiful luminous face. Almost immediately I formed an attachment to him. During that first meeting I met his eldest son, Sayyid Ali. He said, "Ali is your brother. Keep company with him."

He had a large family and I came to know all his sons but I spent more time with Sayyid Ali, who owned a successful construction supply business in Bab Makkah. My first place of work in Saudi Arabia was in Bab Makkah around the corner from the Al-Haddad store and I would often visit. When the time of Hajj arrived during my first months in Saudi Arabia, I was invited to join Al-Haddad's entourage. He performed Hajj every year with his disciples.

On the day of Arafat I set off alone from our family house in the district of Jarwal, taking a taxi to the edge of the plain of Arafat and, following the instructions I had been given, tracked down Al-Haddad's encampment. Hajj fell in the middle of summer. In those days tents were not air-conditioned and the heat was oppressive but this only seemed to heighten the spiritual intensity of this gathering of Sufis within the greater gathering of Muslims on the most sacred plain on the most sacred day of the year. Al-Haddad sat amidst dozens of his disciples in a state of extreme awe. He spoke with grave adoration of the Day of Arafat and its significance. He instructed everyone in the assembly to recite *Sura Ikhlas* one thousand times. This, he said, was important. He then withdrew as, individually, we all began reciting the heaviest and most powerful Sura of the Holy Qur'an through the day. I recited *Sura Ikhlas* on the Mount of Mercy, walking back through throngs of worshippers and in Al-Haddad's tent. At that point I was unfamiliar with most of his disciples but knew Sayyid Hadi Al-Haddar, who I had met in London. I kept close to him. Habib presided over meals which, in the light of Arafat and his presence, seemed sanctified.

I continued to visit Al-Haddad after the Hajj. He spent half his year in Mombasa and the other half living with his sons in Jeddah. Born in Qaydun, a small town in Hadramaut, he was a Sayyid, a direct descendent of the Prophet Mohamed, peace and blessings be upon him. His lineage traced back to Sayyid-ina Husayn, the Messenger's grandson. The Husayni Sharifs of South Yemen were known as the Bani 'Alawi, named after Imam 'Alawi, the grandson of Ahmad Al-Muhajir, who settled in Hadramaut in the fourth century of Hijra. The Sayyids of the

Bani 'Alawi (*Saadatu l'Alawiyya*) established one of the world's oldest, most enduring and most cosmopolitan Sufi orders. Committed to scholarship, spiritual practice and travel, they spread the traditional practice of Islam throughout the world, to India, Southeast Asia and Africa. Habib Al-Haddad was the spiritual heir of his great ancestor, the celebrated 18th century Sufi saint, Imam Abdullah ibn 'Alawi Al-Haddad, may God be well pleased with them both.

He memorized the Qur'an at an early age and studied Arabic and the religious sciences and was placed under spiritual discipline. My teacher, Sayyid Omar Abdullah, who knew him when he was young, told me that as a youth his extreme good looks combined with intense spirituality made him so physically attractive that he was forced to veil his face in public.

He also had, from a young age, a profound *kashf* or unveiling. Sayyid Omar Abdullah once told me that when he was a student in England, Al-Haddad sent him a letter, which he ended by blessing him in a series of seemingly unrelated destinations in Europe, the Middle East and Africa beginning with London and ending in Zanzibar. As it turned out, months later Sayyid Omar travelled to each of these destinations in the exact sequence listed in the letter. Of Al-Haddad's *kashf*, Sayyid Omar mentioned an incident he witnessed with one of the Shaykh's most advanced disciples, who also had a great sense of humor. Sayyid Omar was sitting with Shaykh and disciple and Al-Haddad said to him with a smile, "You know your spiritual station would be raised if you would only make *ghusl* (full ritual ablution) after you have sex with your wife and before you sleep." His disciple burst into laughter and said, "Habib, do me a favor. Confine your *kashf* to the sitting room and *stay out of my bedroom!*"

He was a disciple of the Hadrami Zanzibarian Sufi master Omar bin Sumait, may God be well pleased with him, and emigrated to East Africa, settling in Mombasa. His influence over Islam in East Africa was immense. He taught Islam and the Sufi sciences and ventured deep into the jungles to reach out to pagan tribes. Through his powerful spirituality, profound wisdom and beautiful character he brought tens of thousands of tribal people to Islam in Africa. In the process he contracted malaria and became lame in one leg from a road accident on one of his safaris into the interior.

In Jeddah, he met his disciples and visitors in a small anteroom off the entrance to the large family home his eldest son Ali built in the early 1980s in the Bani Malek district. The room was lined with books and furnished unpretentiously with Belgian carpets and plush floor cushions and bolsters.

He would descend from his living quarters in the morning and sit with visitors until the noon prayers, after which he would share the noonday meal (*ghada*) with whoever was present and retire for an afternoon rest (*qaylula*). He would return for the afternoon prayer and sit with visitors through the sunset and night prayers and the evening meal (*asha*) after which he would retire. He kept to this taxing schedule into his late 80s, until his health drastically weakened.

Visitors from around the world would come to call. Day after day he would minister to a parade of ordinary and extraordinary people, hearing their problems, patiently giving good counsel and always remembering God. Conversation in his presence flowed from the mundane to the divine. Every gathering was organic and natural yet infused with Al-Haddad's transcendent presence.

I remember sitting beside him as one of his disciples went over in excruciating detail his problem of finding another flat in Jeddah. Al-Haddad listened to him patiently, giving him sincere advice on where to go and what to do. I kept thinking to myself, "What a waste of this great saint's time!" How little I understood. On another occasion, toward the end of an evening after the Night prayer, one of Al-Haddad's Hadrami disciples turned up suddenly and Habib upbraided him sharply. "What's the matter with you? It's late. You shouldn't come here so late." I looked on in reproachful silence. The next day I saw the same man sitting before Habib, who was holding his head between his hands speaking to him with great love and compassion.

One day I was sitting in Al-Haddad's house with Sayyid Omar. We were in a room adjacent to Al-Haddad's anteroom where he was meeting one of his disciples. I thought how exhausting it must be for him to have to interact with the usual assortment of self-involved, worldly people like me and feeling more than a little guilty for taking up his time. I said to Sayyid Omar, "I don't understand how someone like Habib can *stand* being around someone like me." Sayyid Omar turned to me and said, "Someone like Habib only wants to be alive *because* of someone like you." He was silent for a moment. "Otherwise, he would rather be with his Lord." This reminded me of a Sufi saying that the Friend of God (*Wali'ullah*) is "the one who lives for his neighbor".

Habib always encouraged moderation and balance in his disciples. This was the way of the Bani 'Alawi. My teacher Sayyid Omar related a story of a young Zanzibarian disciple of Habib Omar bin Sumait who had decided to emigrate to Europe. He asked his Shaykh for spiritual permission (*ijaza*) to perform an intensive course of invocation and was refused. Habib Omar bin Sumait explained that in a place like Europe, which is materialistic and permeated with forgetfulness (*ghaflah*), the impact of invoking God was far more powerful than in places where invocation and prayer were common. The disciple immigrated to Europe but failed to heed his Shaykh's admonition and performed long, intensive spiritual practices, which made him lose his mind.

I was acquainted with an extraordinary Saudi Sufi acolyte who followed a great shaykh from Mauritania. He was one of the most impressive disciples I have ever met, incredibly intense with a single-minded devotion to the path of invocation. He was so intense, so devoted, so superior to me that he made me uncomfortable. If I had learned anything over my years on the Path it was that the process was natural and gradual. There was intensity, to be sure, but the intensity was reflective, self-effacing and all the great Sufis I had ever met had a sense of humor and the ability to laugh and enjoy life even as they remembered God. This *faqir* was just too serious.

One day I visited him at his home. He was suddenly acting erratically, formulating grandiose, messianic plans for a new utopian spiritual society. It was as if he had experienced a personality change. The whole encounter was slightly mad. How could this extraordinary disciple go haywire in this way? I had seen this behavior before and came away from the meeting very disturbed and decided to avoid his company. From mutual acquaintances I learned that he experienced a complete mental breakdown. My intuition had been right.

Sometime later I walked into Al-Haddad's *majlis*. The Saudi disciple was sitting in the presence of Habib. He was like a shipwreck washed up on shore. Habib was leaning over to him, speaking with great compassion, advising him, reciting invocations and healing the sincere disciple, who eventually found his equilibrium.

The *tariqa* of the *Saadatu l'Alawiyya* was a path of knowledge. Gatherings revolved around open-ended spiritual conversation. Being accustomed to the more ritualistic Shadhiliyya way, I found the informal and intellectual gatherings at Habib's challenging. Even my brilliant, scholarly Arabist friend Abdal Hakim Murad (T.J. Winter) complained that he sometimes found it difficult to follow the spiritual conversation carried out in the presence of the Shaykh, which shifted seamlessly from classical Arabic to local Hadrami idioms and back.

I had been used to the practice of the Shadhiliyya Sufi orders, which revolved around the rituals of reciting from the *diwans*, performing the *hadra* and listening to discourse. Having weak Arabic, it was hard to follow Habib's gatherings although at times, his Arabic was so clear that I could follow every word.

I often felt outmatched and discouraged and I mentioned this to Al-Haddad. He prescribed for me the supplication of the Prophet Moses, peace be upon him, from the Holy Qur'an to recite as a *dhikr* to help improve my Arabic.

Rabbi ishrah li sadri
wa yassir li amri
wa ahlul l'uqdata min lisani
yafqahu qawli.
(My Lord expand my breast for me,
Ease my task for me,
And remove the impediment from my tongue,
So that they understand me.)*

After I began repeating this *ayat* there were many subsequent occasions when I could understand his spiritual conversation with uncanny clarity.

So, while I would visit Habib in Jeddah semi-regularly, my relationship with the Shaykh remained informal for several years. I frankly preferred the company of my mentor Sayyid Omar Abdullah, who taught me in his beautiful, rich English.

At one point I let myself become completely caught up in my work and family life and kept putting off a visit to the house in Bani Malek. One day, finally, I decided to force myself to make a long overdue visit. When I arrived in Bani Malek and knocked on the door, one of the female members of the household answered and told me that Habib was at the airport, preparing to depart for Kenya. Suddenly, I was overcome with remorse. I had wasted six months and the opportunity to sit with one of the world's greatest living saints.

I drove straight to the airport, parked and rushed into the terminal reception area. To my relief I found Habib sitting with his sons, grandsons and disciples amidst the rows of seats for waiting passengers while he was checked in to the flight. I rushed over to him, kissed his hand and his forehead, on the verge of tears. I told him I was so sorry I did not see him this time. "I feel very terrible, very upset that I didn't visit you." He held my

---

* *Sura Taha*, 20:25-28, translation by Nawawi Foundation

hand with great compassion and said, "Don't worry Haroon, I am always with you and you are always with me." I was deeply moved and comforted and vowed that I would not make the same mistake again. I sat with Habib until he had to move into the departure lounge. I accepted his comforting words as a sign of his immense kindness and compassion.

Sometime later I mentioned my airport exchange with Al-Haddad to Sayyid Omar Abdullah, by way of saying that he was very kind and compassionate to me and, to my surprise, Sayyid Omar stopped, looked at me gravely and said, "Did he really say this to you?" Yes, I said. Sayyid Omar then said, "He wasn't being kind or compassionate. No Shaykh can say this except with Divine authority. This means that he is your Shaykh in the unseen and has always been your Shaykh."

There is a consensus on this matter among all the masters of the Way, which was clearly articulated by the great Shadhili Shaykh Abu'l Abbas Al-Mursi,who said, "No Master makes himself known to disciples unless he has been led to do so by inspirations (*waridat*) and unless he has received authorization of God and of His Messenger."

Finally, after years of vacillation and delay, I came to Habib Ahmed Mashhur and asked to take his hand. He said, in a matter-of-fact way, "We have been waiting." He initiated me into the *tariqa* and prescribed the *Wird Al-Latif* for recitation in the morning and the *Ratib Al-Haddad* for recitation in the evening. He sealed the initiation by saying simply, "Now I am your Shaykh." That evening he hosted a meal to celebrate my entry into the *tariqa*. It was an honor I had done nothing to deserve.

When he was in Jeddah I continued visiting my Shaykh alone or with Sayyid Omar Abdullah. At any given time there would be visitors from all parts of the world but there were rarely ever more than about 20 men in attendance. It was a sign of the times. One day we had been at a gathering with Al-Haddad at the home of one of his disciples and had returned to Bani Malek. As a group of us were entering the Al-Haddad house and my companion, Mostafa Al-Badawi, casually observed, "You know, in another age, thousands would have been sitting at his feet instead of our small group."

Whenever Habib left for Kenya it was the custom of his followers to see him off at King Khaled International Airport in Jeddah. On one of these occasions I walked with him as he moved from his car into the terminal. At every step of the way, a disciple or admirer approached to say farewell. Dozens came to pay their respects. It was an extraordinary sight. In Saudi Arabia Sufism was banned and displays of reverence to a Shaykh of Instruction were forcibly discouraged. In another time and place Habib's departure would have been attended by hundreds, if not thousands of disciples. This informal, surreptitious procession was, in a way, even more impressive.

I met several times with him in private or with members of my family. He gave my wife a *wird* to perform and met with my mother, who had converted to Islam and was visiting from California. He gave her an invocation to recite and answered her questions. After she left, Habib looked at me, shook his head with a sad smile and said, "*Miskeena* (poor woman), she has *was-was* (uncontrolled thoughts, whisperings)." This was true and plagued my mother until her death, may God be merciful to her. However, she died in a state of extreme grace, was buried as a Muslim and I believe her meeting with Al-Haddad played a part in her blessed passing.

He was robust and normally full of energy but periodically he would suffer a relapse of malaria, which he had picked up many years before in East Africa, and would withdraw until he recovered. On several occasions he said to me, "Haroon I have been suffering from malaria, please pray for me."

The first Gulf War, "Desert Storm", was a metaphysical turning point. When Saudi and American armed forces joined to fight the Iraqi army, Muslim against Muslim, Habib Al-Haddad withdrew into spiritual retreat for the duration of the conflict. We did not see him for weeks.

From that point on he became increasingly frail. Yet he continued to descend from his apartments and preside over gatherings after the sunset prayers. During Ramadan he led the *tarawih* prayers every evening. Finally, in his late 80s his health gave out altogether. He lost the use of his legs, then his eyesight and hearing. He was no longer able to come down to meet visitors. From time to time we would ascend to see him. I missed him but didn't want to tire him. At one time I came with my son Abu Bakr to visit. His grandson Sayyid Adnan bin Ali, who had served Habib throughout his youth, brought me up to his apartments. He was reclining, immobile and blind. Adnan whispered in his grandfather's ear, "Haroon is here." Habib couldn't acknowledge my presence but he was a river of invocation and Qur'an. I listened and invoked God and prayed for my Shaykh and for myself and my children.

On another occasion I was sitting alone in his small study. Suddenly Sayyid Adnan brought his grandfather into the room in a wheel chair. He whispered my name in his ear before leaving me alone with him. He was extremely weak. I couldn't be sure whether he really knew I was there. I sat on the floor at his feet. I remembered the magnificent, vigorous and compassionate wise man I had known and I wept. I wept for all the lost opportunities I had to benefit from his presence. I wept for his awesome humility. I wept in gratitude to God that I had been given the gift of knowing him. I wept for the love of him and for all my many flaws that he overlooked. I wept for a long time, wrapped in his presence, and although he never uttered a word or acknowledged me in any way, I felt that he had spoken to me with love, directly, clearly, deeply, forcefully, straight to my heart.

A short time later I heard that his condition had suddenly deteriorated and he had been admitted into intensive care. I drove to the hospital, hoping to see him. Sayyid Ali came out to greet me. "*Miskeen*," (Poor soul) he said with a sad smile. Then he added, "He's nearly 90." I said, "He has had a long life. May God cover him with His Mercy."

It was late on Wednesday night on the 7 December 1995 (14 Rajab 1416) when I received a call that Habib Ahmed Mashhur Al-Haddad had passed away in the late afternoon and that he would be buried in Al-Maala cemetery in Makkah al-Mukaramah after the dawn prayers. I arrived at Al-Maala after dawn prayers to find the cemetery empty. I waited outside, near the grave of my mother-in-law who was buried near the grave of Sayyidat Khadijah at Hejoun and prayed for her and for my Shaykh and to be allowed to pray the funeral (*janazah*) prayers for him.

I returned to my home and picked up my eldest son, Muhsin. The two of us returned to the Holy Mosque and stationed ourselves in the shade of the Sinan Pasha domes between the Yemeni Corner and the Black Stone. Prior to the noon prayers in the Holy Mosque, I scanned the *mataf* for members of the family or followers but could find no one. I vowed to attend every prayer in the Holy Mosque until the *janazah* prayer for Habib was performed. After the noon prayers the *salat al-mawt* (Prayer for the Dead) was called and believers clustered beside the Kaaba in the bright winter sunlight to pray for the deceased. We rushed out of the shade across the *mataf* toward the jostling crowd behind the imam and heard the murmur of Habib's name.

The *janazah* prayer was performed and Habib Ahmad Mashhur Al-Haddad was lifted above the throngs on a wooden bier covered in a green banner embroidered with yellow calligraphy. The crowd surged toward the *mas'a* (the track between the mounts of Safa and Marwa) carrying the body of the Shaykh aloft and reciting the *tahlil* (the Muslim confession of faith) with increasing force. We carried Al-Haddad across the *mas'a*, up the steps, out through the piazza area, passing into the *Souq al-Lail*. The passion of the *tahlil* intensified as the procession crowd increased in number and I recalled the verse from a *qasida* of Shaykh Mohamed ibn Al-Habib:

"You are a treasure to My worshippers,
you are a dhikr for mankind."

The bier came to rest at the enclosure that was reserved for 'Alawi Sayyids. The crowd of worshippers lowered the shrouded body of the saint to rest in a simple, unmarked grave. We all wept. My son told me many years later that he had never seen me weep so much. I saw Sayyid Ali, we were both in tears. We embraced. I can't imagine what this loss was for him. We recited Qur'an and other invocations. The burial ground was charged with light. This was a day of passing. The world that we knew would never be the same.

One of the *awliya* recommended that when praying one should always picture the Kaaba and one's Shaykh standing before the Kaaba. I have never been able to picture anyone but Al-Haddad in my mind's eye standing before the House of God. I see him in my prayers. I see him easily. I carry him in my heart.

**"Oh God! Guide me to one
who can guide me to You!
Cause me to reach one
who will cause me to reach You!"**

**A supplication for the seeker
from Shaykh 'Abd Al-Qadir 'Isa***

* The Realities of Sufism, translated by Suraqah Abdul Aziz.

AMBASSADOR EXTRAORDINAIRE AND PLENIPOTENTIARY

In the popular mind love is usually linked with romance and sex. I never imagined that the first person I would fall madly in love with would be a short, flamboyant, erudite, bespectacled, snaggle-toothed black man from Zanzibar who spilled things, wore long coats over a sarong, spoke in rich Edwardian English, had an infectious laugh and walked with a cane. It was through him I understood the meaning of the declaration of the Companions of the Prophet Mohamed, peace and blessings be upon him, "May my mother and father be sacrificed for you!" I never understood how anyone could say that about their parents until I met Sayyid Omar Abdullah.

From the moment I laid eyes on him I fell in love with him. I can say that I loved him more than anyone else in my life. He taught me the meaning of love and its reciprocity. He knew I loved him and I knew he loved me. My heart surged when I knew I would see him. I missed him terribly when he was away. I thought about him constantly. I enjoyed every moment I had with him. He was a kind of *uberfather* for me. He was my best friend. I felt safe knowing he was in the world. When he died, I was desolate, overcome with a sense of profound loss from which I have never fully recovered.

As I came to know him I discovered that I was not the only one who had fallen in love with him. Once we were walking together on the streets of old Jeddah in Saudi Arabia, and someone approached us. He came up to Sayyid Omar and cried out in Arabic, "*Ya Habib*! (Habib is an honorific the people of Hadramaut in South Yemen – *Hadaram* – bestow upon their spiritual elders) I love you!" Then he asked, "Why do I love you, Habib?" Sayyid Omar lowered his eyes, smiling, and shook his head modestly. "A gift from my Lord," he shrugged. I witnessed this kind of exchange many times. The great Sufi and Proof of Islam, Imam Abu Hamid Al-Ghazali wrote that one of the marks of honor bestowed upon the people who have attained knowledge on the path to God is that they are beloved of all creatures. Sayyid Omar elicited love wherever he went.

When I first met him he was serving as 'Ambassador Extraordinaire and Plenipotentiary' from Comoros Islands, which, I think meant that he was the little island nation's only ambassador. He travelled the world on behalf of Comoros and, through his charisma, managed to bring the country many millions of dollars in foreign aid, particularly from the Gulf countries, where he was especially beloved.

Beneath his diplomatic cover he was one of the greatest living African educators and beneath his educational cover, he was a Sufi saint. While on one of his diplomatic missions, he came to learn of a young group of Sufi acolytes living in London and he came to pay us a visit.

He was a force of nature and took our group by storm. He savored knowledge as if he was feasting at a table groaning with delicacies. Indeed, he often said that Sufism was about taste. "Without tasting the sweetness of *dhikr* and knowledge it is very difficult to continue on the Path." There was no subject off limits. He laughed easily. His laughter was infectious, his sense of humor contagious. His knowledge of the path was encyclopedic. I had never heard anyone deliver classical Sufi doctrine in English with such clarity and depth of insight and with such boisterous good humor. The atmosphere was charged in his presence. He exuded an intense joy of life. He loved people. He came with his close companion Sayyid Hadi Al-Haddar. The two of them sat cross-legged on the floor with us and spoke of Sufi doctrine and practice. Sayyid Hadi, who was an ecstatic, solemnly announced to the group, "I congratulate myself for being among you." Sayyid Omar balanced sobriety and intoxication, and combined his magnetism with a rich eloquence. He galvanized his listeners with insights, anecdotes and wisdom sayings. As he spoke his embroidered cap (*kufia*) would begin slipping farther and farther to the back of his head. Just before it fell off altogether Sayyid Omar would rescue it and slide it up back to the top of his smooth head and continue talking.

When the time for prayer came I leapt at the chance to help him make his ritual ablutions. I filled a pitcher and poured water for him in my upstairs room. He invoked a blessing on me. While we were having tea after dinner Sayyid Omar addressed me. He asked me where I was from. I had been an actor in Hollywood before I entered the path. I had been in the theater since I was a small child. I thought that the only thing I wanted in life was to be a great performer. I left what looked to be a promising career, suddenly and, for my family and friends, dramatically. I joined a Sufi order and never looked back, or so I imagined. I told him I was from America. He asked me what state I was from. I answered that I was from California. He then grinned and burst out suddenly with, "So you left *Hollywood* and came *here!*" I turned beet red. He had nailed me. The whole assembly exploded into laughter. My friends all knew my past. I realized that I was carrying this mythology around with me about having been an actor in Hollywood and left it all for the Path. In one funny and embarrassing (for me at least) moment, he put that pretention to rest.

This was the first time I had ever interacted with someone

possessed of spiritual insight, or *firasah*, although I had always been fascinated by this capacity, which is a combination of innate ability enhanced by intense invocation. The Prophet Mohamed, peace and blessings be upon him, said, "Fear the insight (*firasah*) of the believer, for he sees with the Light of God."

On another occasion Sayyid Omar suddenly appeared at the *zawiya*. It was an afternoon. I was sitting with a friend of mine who had just returned from many months in Palestine under the tutelage of a Sufi shaykh who had put him under an incredibly intense regime of invocation that had left him in a highly strung state. He had returned to England and was at loose ends.

There were only two of us alone in the *minzah* when Sayyid Omar appeared. He strode into the *zawiya* and, without pause or ceremony, sat directly in front of my friend, greeting him and asking his name. "Abdul Latif", my friend replied. "Well Abdul Latif, I must warn you, you mustn't try to go too fast." Abdul Latif listened, nonplussed. Sayyid Omar continued, gravely but gently, "Because if you go too fast you might lose your balance." Abdul Latif was speechless. He'd just received a rather alarming admonition from an exotic older gentleman he'd never laid eyes on. He stared back, dumbstruck. Sayyid Omar looked him in the eyes and said, "You know what I mean," then casually added, "What do you do? Do you cook?" Stunned, my friend nodded, stammering, "Uh, yes, I...I cook at The Buttery at the John Slade Art School in East London." This was Sayyid Omar's way of letting him know that he wasn't just whistling Dixie; that he could see into his heart. He then said again for emphasis, "Don't try to go too fast. Take things slowly and you will be fine." My friend took his advice and has kept on the path up to now, never losing his balance.

I witnessed this kind of exchange numerous times and was fascinated by these flashes of insight he seemed suddenly and without warning to blurt out. When I mentioned this, he said innocently, "Do I really?" He explained that things just came to him suddenly and he was impelled to say something. It was

150

intuitive rather than cognitive. He dismissed this faculty as of little importance.

Born in Zanzibar in 1918, he was of Hadrami extraction and could trace his lineage directly back to the Prophet Mohamed, peace and blessings be upon him, through the great Sufi Shaykh Habib Abu Bakr bin Salem, making him a Sayyid. He was raised in a Sufi family from the *Saadatu l'Alawiyya* Sufi order of Hadramaut. He was one of the most educated men in Africa. A graduate of Makerere University in Uganda, in the early 1950s he took a degree in Islamic and Comparative Law from the School of Oriental and African Studies in London. During this period he came to know the British Sufi scholar and author, Martin Lings, who was a fellow student.

When Sayyid Omar returned from England in the 1950s, he served as chancellor of Zanzibar's prestigious Islamic Academy. He returned to England in 1960 to earn an advanced degree in Comparative Religion and Philosphy from Oxford University. His master's thesis at Oxford was on "The Concept of Felicity in Medaeval Islamic Philosophy". In 1964, one year after he returned to Zanzibar, the Government of Sultan Jamshid bin Abdullah was overthrown by African revolutionaries. In the aftermath of the revolution all those associated with the previous regime were under threat. Hundreds were killed. Although he had no political affiliations and his presence was never less than benign, Sayyid Omar's life was in danger.Within days of the revolution he was warned that he would be arrested. He gathered up his family and left Zanzibar, taking asylum in the Comoros Islands.

His standing was so high in Africa that he was immediately given citizenship and became a government advisor and the country's roving ambassador. He was a disciple of the great East African Hadrami Sufi master Habib Omar bin Sumait. He once confessed to me that he turned down the opportunity to remain in England and earn his doctorate because he was too attached to his Shaykh. He said, "I wasn't a very good *murid* (disciple) but

151

I loved being with my Shaykh too much." He said this to me, I knew, because I was, indeed, a very poor disciple but loved his company more than anything. I don't believe for a minute that Sayyid Omar wasn't a great *murid*.

He never stopped travelling. A poem was written about him calling him *Al-Rahhal*, "The Wanderer". A friend once told me that the people of the East African coast (*Sawahel - Swahilis*) loved two things more than anything else: *safari* (travel) and resting. In this sense, Sayyid Omar was a typical Swahili. He loved travelling. He would go anywhere at the drop of a hat. And he loved to rest. I would ask him if he would like to go to such and such a place and, without a moment's hesitation he would always say "*Yala!*" (Let's go!). When we would take off by car he would begin to invoke the names of God and almost immediately fall asleep. He told me many times, "I never regret any sleep that I have." His reasoning was that when one is sleeping there is no *hisab*, or accounting, by God. Sleep is a recess from judgment.

Sometime after my first meeting with Sayyid Omar I had a vivid dream or *ru'ya*. In it he was standing before me. I said to him, apropos of nothing in particular, "The thing is, I can fly." He didn't speak but, rather, made an upward sweep of his arm as if to say, "So fly!" And I did. I began to fly, rising above him as he gestured me higher and higher. I kept rising until Sayyid Omar was a tiny speck and the atmosphere became so rarified that I lost consciousness. When I regained consciousness in my dream I was standing in front of my own personal Kaaba. It was smaller than the real Kaaba but very beautiful and powerful. I made *takbir* (opening the prayer by raising one's hands and declaring "*Allahu Akbar*" - "God is Great") and said my prayers. I had no idea what the meaning of the dream was but it was one of the most beautiful and vibrant dreams I have ever had.

A short time later, I was introduced to the woman who became my wife. She was from Makkah Al-Mukarramah. Her father was a *mutawif*, or pilgrim guide, and she grew up in Al-Jiyad, across the street from the Kaaba. We married but did not settle in Saudi Arabia for three years. There were some legal problems that kept us away from the country. I longed to visit Makkah, to make *Hajj* and *Umrah*, to see the Holy Kaaba with my eyes.

After my wife and I were married, we lived for a time in Egypt and then we moved to California. During that period, I had another dream in which Sayyid Omar appeared. At this point I had not seen him for years. In the dream I was standing near the Mount of Safa in the *mas'a* (the track between the mounts of Safa and Marwa) within the Holy Mosque in Makkah. I had never been to Makkah at this point and I had never seen the *mas'a*, even in photographs. I had no idea what it looked like in real life. But here I was in my dream, wrapped in *ihram* at the foot of the mount of Safa. The atmosphere was crowded and effulgent. From out of the crowd, Sayyid Omar emerged. He approached me, smiling, gestured and said my Muslim name, "Haroon". That was all. When finally I did arrive in Makkah and made *umrah* (the lesser pilgramage) and performed the *sa'ee* (the ritual of seven circuits between the mounts of Safa and Marwa) for the first time, it was exactly as I had seen it in the dream. And still later I performed *umrah* with Sayyid Omar many times, standing in exactly the same spot as I had in my dream.

We eventually settled in Makkah and I was blessed to reside for 23 years within the precincts of this sacred city and God, in His Infinite Generosity, has allowed me to continue visiting His House, even though I have done nothing to deserve this blessing and remain completely unworthy of any of the gifts I have received.

Once we had settled in Saudi Arabia, I searched for other Sufis. Although I found isolated *fuqara* living in Makkah, the only regular circle of remembrance I discovered was held in Jeddah by Omar Kamel, the brother of Saudi tycoon Saleh Kamel. Although anyone could attend, this was a rich man's gathering, held in a special courtyard attached to Omar's mansion in Jeddah. It was pleasant, the food was excellent and, from time to time a truly great Sufi would attend. But, unlike the gatherings I had grown accustomed to in Morocco, Egypt, and elsewhere, these assemblies were mild, tentative and self-conscious. This was to some extent because the practice of Sufism was suppressed by the religious authorities in Saudi Arabia. The Sufi traditions of *majlis* (gatherings of invocation) and *mawlid* (celebrations of the Prophet Mohamed, peace be upon him) had been largely eradicated. Moreover, since the uprising in the Holy Mosque of Makkah in 1979, all religious gatherings of any kind were more or less forbidden or at least closely watched.

Every evening after the *majlis*, Omar's rich business friends would sit on raised benches (*dhikkas*) and talk about business, their travels, deluxe hotels they stayed in and restaurants in Europe they dined at. They were decent and devout men with the best of intentions, but the gatherings were a dim shadow of the true Sufi *majalis*. And I am eternally grateful for them because, it was on one of these nights that I was re-united with Sayyid Omar.

I saw him sitting in the assembly. At first I thought I might be hallucinating. When I realized he really was present, I rushed over to sit down beside him. I reminded him of our meeting in London years before and told him about my dreams. When I told him about flying he said with typical modesty, "You are lucky. I wish I could fly." From that moment we were inseparable whenever he was in Saudi Arabia.

He was still, at that point, serving the Comorean government, by this time as an adviser to the President, Ahmed Abdullah, who had seized power in a *coup d'etat* led by French mercenaries. However, his relations with Abdullah were not good and, although he never said anything directly about the president, he clearly held a very low opinion of him. Once when I was sitting with Habib Ahmed Mashhur Al-Haddad, he mentioned that Ahmed Abdullah was one of his disciples. I reported this to Sayyid Omar and he replied dryly, "He's lucky that Habib considers him a disciple". Ahmed Abdullah was subsequently killed in another *coup d'etat*.

Eventually Sayyid Omar left government service and took a position with the World Muslim League as a roving emissary. He was recommended to the post by Prince Saud Al-Faisal, the long-serving Saudi Foreign Minister, who had known Sayyid Omar when he was the Comorean Ambassador. He took the job to support his family. He never asked anyone for anything, yet many of his followers would give him gifts of money. He never spent any money on himself but saved everything he was given by admirers to provide for his family. I was once helping him get ready for travel, sorting through his documents and personal effects and discovered thousands of dollars worth of currency in many denominations, in wads of cash, stuffed into his pockets, wallet and suitcase. He never touched any of this money. He built a two-story house in Moroni for his wife. He rarely spent any time himself living in it. He was always in a state of travel. He had two daughters. One lived in Jeddah with her Tanzanian husband, Dr. Omar Saleh, who was a very kind and gentle physician employed at Bugshan Hospital.

Once Sayyid Omar came to learn a wealthy admirer had given him money that had been allocated for *zakat*, the obligatory tax on wealth meant to be distributed to the poor. While he was far from affluent, Sayyid Omar was also not poor. He was very upset when he discovered this and took all the money, which was a rather large sum, and distributed it to the poor. I remember that this was the only time I actually saw him visibly unsettled. He couldn't wait to rid himself of this money, which he considered to be unlawful.

It was my great good fortune that he would come to Saudi Arabia and stay for months at a time. When he was in Makkah, he would stay at my home. We turned our living room into his bedroom when he was with us. I spent every available moment with him. In the years that I was with him I learned as much from his presence and behavior as from his words.

I never saw him lose his temper. Actually, I did, once...sort of. We were standing in a crowd waiting for an office building to

155

open in Jeddah and a rude young man pushed his way roughly through the crowd, knocking everyone in his path aside. To my astonishment, Sayyid Omar ripped into the fellow, rebuking him for his bad behavior. I'd never seen him do anything like that in all the years I'd been with him. He must have noticed my surprise because when he turned to me he smiled, and without a trace of ire, said, "Imam Shafi'i said, 'He who is made angry and doesn't get angry is a donkey.'"

He never spoke ill of anyone, although at times he would make it clear that he didn't care for someone. If asked whether he wanted to see a particular person that he did not have a high regard for he would respond with a terse and final "No." That was as negative as he ever got.

He was one of the most patient men I have ever known. He would sometimes wait for a year before receiving his salary from the World Muslim League. I used to take him to World Muslim League headquarters in Makkah to try and collect what was owed to him. He would sit patiently for day after day after day, always pleasant, never losing his temper. He was run from pillar to post and yet he never complained and was always polite and respectful to everyone he dealt with.

His beautiful character, knowledge, charm and sophistication gained him acceptance in any company. Even the *Salafiya* (the followers of Mohamed ibn Abdul Wahhab and Ibn Taymiyya who dominate religious life in Saudi Arabia and some other Gulf countries and reject the practice of Sufism) embraced him.

Sayyid Omar was the most eloquent living interpreter of classical Sufi doctrine in the English language and he was a tremendous conversationalist. Yet he never left a gathering without repeating the Prophet's invocation: *Subhanaka Allahumma wa bi Hamdika Wash-hadu an la ilaha illa anta astaghfiruka wa atoobu ilayk.* ("Glory be to You O God, and Praise to You and I witness that there is no god but You. I ask your forgiveness and I turn to you.") Of this invocation the Prophet, peace be upon him, said: "Whosoever is sitting in a company and indulges in much idle talk, but before rising says…, his talk shall be forgiven." I found this to be one of his most impressive qualities. He never forgot that he was in the presence of God. For 30 years I have tried to follow his example, but I still find it a struggle to retain the awareness of God to remember this simple invocation after engaging in conversation.

If he had a consistent message it was one of tolerance, for human frailty, for other beliefs, for weakness and wrong action in others. He once said, "You have to be very careful about defining someone as an unbeliever (*kafir*). A *kafir* is someone who has received the Message, *understood* it and then rejected it. Most non-Muslims have not received the Message, fewer still understand it. Even many Muslims haven't received and understood the Message."

We were sitting together once and he said, "If you read the Qur'an with great care, you will understand that most people go to Paradise." He gave everybody a way in. We once sent him to America on a speaking tour, which was very successful. After one of his talks, a young American woman came up to him and said, "I love what you said and I think I should become a Muslim but, you see, I'm a stripper." Without missing a beat Sayyid Omar grinned and said, "Well, don't let that stop you." She said happily, "Yes, I'll become a Muslim and then I know I'll give it up." He didn't admonish her for what she was doing, but encouraged her to something better.

He once said, "Westerners have the greatest capacity to accept and follow the Path in our time because they have no preconceptions, they understand the value of time and they use their intellect. The only thing they have going against them is that they have built up bad habits." I found this to be true. While it was easy for me to comprehend and accept Sufi doctrine and practice the discipline (*suluk*), I felt weighed down by deeply ingrained impulses from my misspent youth. Habib Omar and I were travelling through the Gulf together. I was away from my wife and, after a time, started to be troubled by lust (*shahwa*). Over dinner one evening I asked him if, as a young man living in Europe, he was ever overcome by feelings of lust, hoping he would give me some advice as to how to deal with this distraction. He looked up and said without hesitation, "No." His upbringing had protected him.

Still, he had incredible empathy for ordinary people. A young Comorean working in Jeddah who knew Sayyid Omar told me that when he gave discourse in Moroni, all the cafés and bars would empty out and throngs of young people would flock to come to hear him speak. He was the spiritual equivalent of a rock star in East Africa.

On another occasion, when he was in London, the Imam of the Regent's Park Mosque called him in a panic. He said, "We have a serious problem and we need your help. We don't know what to do! Can you come with us?" They took Sayyid Omar to Harley Street to the office of a physician. He was an older man, in his late fifties. Habib sat down with him and said, "How can I help you?" The physician said, "Over the years I have treated many Muslims and, through them, have come to love and respect Islam and I believe it is true and I believe I should become a Muslim." Sayyid Omar said, "That is very good. So what's the problem?" The Imam looked to Sayyid Omar as if to say, "Just wait until you hear this." The physician responded, "Well, I know that a Muslim is expected to pray five times a day. But I am old and set in my ways and I am very busy with my practice. In all honesty I can't guarantee that I will be able to keep to the five prayers." Sayyid Omar said, "Go on." The physician continued, "Also, I know that one is expected to fast the month of Ramadan. I simply can't perform the fast." The Imam looked to Sayyid Omar as if to say, "You see what I mean?" Sayyid Omar said, "Is there anything else?" The good doctor said, "Yes. For the last 30 years every evening I have a glass of sherry. I know this is frivolous and I know that Muslims are not permitted to drink but I honestly don't think I can give up my glass of sherry in the evening. I'm sorry." Sayyid Omar said, "Is there anything else?" The doctor said, "No, I think that's about it. What do you advise?" Sayyid Omar said, "There are many Muslims who fail to perform the five prayers and who don't fast the month of Ramadan and there are many Muslims who drink alcohol and there have been since the time of the Prophet Mohamed, peace and blessings be upon him. These are men and women who were born as Muslims, who believe in Islam and who are accepted as Muslims so my advice is to accept Islam and do the best that you can. You are welcome in Islam." The good doctor became a Muslim.

In Sufi literature, in the *diwans* of the saints, in circles of knowledge, there is much talk of very advanced spiritual states, of annihilation in God (*fanafillah*), of subsistence in God (*baqabillah*), of exalted stations (*maqamat*) and illuminations. I felt that much of this was lost on me. When I was young I never imagined that I could possibly attain these spiritual heights. So I asked Sayyid Omar why it was that we are encouraged to desire knowledge that seems to be out of reach for most people. He replied that God is so immensely generous that He gives His servants everything that they ask for, even if only at the moment of death. He would relate the saying of his shaykh regarding the acquisition of spiritual knowledge: "The later, the better."

He took me everywhere with him, into the presence of some of the greatest saints of the time. Without being in his company I could never have had access to these men.

I would accompany Sayyid Omar on visits to the great Makkan Sufi educator and spiritual guide Sayyid Mohamed Alawi Maliki, who was the son of the Sufi shaykh Sayyid Alawi Maliki. Sayyid Mohamed Alawi had a huge following in Saudi Arabia and across Southeast Asia and elsewhere but he was anathema to the Wahhabi establishment who managed to have him relieved of his teaching post at Umm Al-Qurra University. Sayyid Mohamed Alawi symbolized everything the *Salafis* loathed. He openly practiced *Tasawwuf*, he was incredibly popular, he wrote books praising the Prophet Mohamed and extolling the virtues of *Mawlid*, or the celebration of the birth of the Prophet

Mohamed. After successfully driving him from his position at Umm Al-Qurra University, the religious establishment sought to have his books banned from Saudi Arabia. They wanted to publicly burn his books. The conflict reached a crisis point and King Fahd felt the need to step in. On one of Sayyid Omar's visits Sayyid Mohamed Alawi confided to him that he had a private meeting with the King, who asked him why he couldn't simply fall into line with what the religious authorities wanted. Sayyid Mohamed Alawi replied that he could not conceal what he knew to be true and made a reasoned argument to the King for his positions. The King said, "I respect your reasoning. The only thing I ask from you is that you refrain from holding public *mawalid*." Sayyid Mohamed 'Alawi agreed to keep his gatherings private. And the King said, "From now on if anyone from the scholars attacks you, tell them that I am your protector."

Through his travels Sayyid Omar had built a network of friends and admirers. Wherever he went people of the Path vied to host him. I felt very lucky that he always chose to stay with me in Makkah. He would often teach me indirectly. I have a tendency to overwork myself into a state of exhaustion and ennui. During one of these periods, Sayyid Omar would muse to no one in particular, "It is amazing how people lose the taste for life by working too much." Once when we were driving between Jeddah and Makkah, I mentioned that I was a follower of the Maliki School (*madhhab*). Sayyid Omar laughed and said, "You don't know enough to have a *madhhab*. Just practice Islam." He would rarely lay claim to knowledge. Instead, he would credit his teachers or the great Sufis in history.

During one Ramadan Sayyid Omar was staying with me in Makkah. I noticed that he was sleeping heavily through the day. At first I put this down to a combination of age, fasting and his celebrated love of sleep, but as the days wore on and he never seemed to revive, I became concerned. I called his son-in-law Dr. Omar Saleh. He asked me to bring his father-in-law in for a checkup. It was then I learned that he had long been suffering from diabetes and had gone into diabetic shock. For all the years I had been with him, he never once mentioned his illness and I realized that he had also not taken care of himself properly. For one thing, in the seething Saudi heat he drank cold soft drinks throughout the day. Once he had recovered I admonished him for drinking sugary drinks. He honestly didn't know that they could be lethal for a diabetic. I bought cases of diet drinks to replace the sugar drinks he liked. This was in the 1980s in Saudi Arabia when diet soft drinks were just being introduced into the market, so it is understandable why he had not really been aware that there was an alternative.

From then on his condition was never far from my thoughts. One of Sayyid Omar's devoted students, Dr. Ali Hassan Mwinyi, was elected President of Tanzania. When the President made an official visit to Saudi Arabia he invited his professor to visit him in the official Guest Palace in Jeddah. The Guest Palace is a strange place. Originally built as an Intercontinental Hotel, it was acquired by the government by order of the King when it came to his attention that the hotel overlooked his offshore island palace then under construction. It was converted to an official guest palace for foreign dignitaries and other government guests. Although designed like a hotel, it was guarded and vacant or seemed so when the two of us passed through security to ascend to the President's suite.

We sat with Dr. Mwinyi, who was very welcoming and who clearly revered Sayyid Omar. The meeting was uneventful but it was, in some sense, a turning point. After his diabetic attack, Sayyid Omar's health began to deteriorate. It wasn't that he became overtly ill, but his energy dwindled and his great joy of life receded. My flat in Makkah occupied the whole top floor of a building without an elevator. Sayyid Omar took longer and longer to negotiate the stairs but he did so without complaint. One evening I noticed that he seemed uncharacteristically pensive and quiet. I said, "Would you like to come out to the roof garden to get some air." He smiled, shook his head and said,

"I've had enough air."

Sayyid Omar travelled back home to Comoros. President Mwinyi invited him to accompany the presidential delegation for the annual pilgrimage. I knew he was coming but wasn't sure when. I waited to hear from him once he arrived. No news came. I became concerned and called his son-in-law Dr. Omar Saleh. He informed me that Sayyid Omar had arrived with the Tanzanian delegation, but had been detained at the Hajj Terminal because he was carrying a Comorean, rather than a Tanzanian, passport. He had been left sitting in the terminal for nearly twenty-four hours and had gone into diabetic shock and had to be admitted to hospital. Dr. Omar told me that he had suffered renal failure and had to have a part of his foot amputated. I was beside myself with anxiety. I wanted to see him. Dr. Omar said that Habib didn't want me to see him in his condition. I had to wait.

When he finally left hospital, I rushed to the apartment of his daughter and son-in-law to wait for him. He arrived from the hospital, smiling weakly. He had become emaciated. We helped him in to the apartment and to bed. I sat with him for a while but he was very weak. I came back to see him. He was still wan and fragile but in good humor. It was the last time I saw him.

He returned home to Comoros. A few months later I learned that Sayyid Omar Abdullah had passed away. I went to see his daughter, who was still in Jeddah. We wept together. I was devastated.

Thousands attended his funeral in Moroni. He was deeply loved. Within a few months his daughter also passed away, from a severe asthma attack. She was so like her father; another trace of him lost.

One year later I was in London and visited the home of one of Sayyid Omar's disciples, Habib Abu Bakr Ba Shuaib, to celebrate a memorial for our shaykh. A long time had passed. I had become accustomed to his loss, or so I thought. We recited the Qur'an. Abu Bakr spoke about Sayyid Omar. While he spoke, without warning, the floodgates opened. I missed him too much. I couldn't contain my grief and loss. I broke down and wept uncontrollably. I couldn't stop. I consumed boxes of tissues. I was overwhelmed by sorrow and the memory of my beloved master.

After Sayyid Omar died I was sitting in the company of Habib Ahmed Mashhur Al-Haddad and his disciples. We were remembering Sayyid Omar and one of the elders said, "Habib Omar, he was a great teacher, a great *da'i* (one who calls people to Islam)." Another gestured to me and said, "Haroon was his close companion." Habib Al-Haddad, who was my Shaykh, turned to me and said, "You know, he was your Shaykh." I nodded. Another looked at me and said with conviction, "You have something from him." I hope so.

A quarter century has passed. I have never recovered. He was the love of my life.

**"Live as long as you want, but you must die; love whatever you want,
but you will become separated from it;
and do what you want,
but you will be repaid for it!"**

Imam Abu Hamid Mohamed Al-Ghazali*

* Letter to a Disciple (*Ayyuha'l-Walad*), translated by Tobias Mayer.

SONG AND DANCE

"What happens in the Circle of Remembrance is not dancing"

Sheikh Muzaffer Ozak Al-Jerrahi*

"Those who call it 'dancing' are utterly wrong. It is a state that cannot be explained in words: 'without experience or knowledge.'"

'Ali 'Uthman Al-Hujwiri**

"When souls tremble, desirous of reunion, Even phantoms dance, oh uncomprehending one!"

Shaykh Abu Madyan Shu'ayb***

* The Unveiling of Love, translated by Muhtar Holland.

** *Kashf Al-Mahjoub*, translated by Reynold A. Nicholson.

*** *Qasida in Nun* from the Way of Abu Madyan, translated by Vincent J. Cornell.

Photo left: Shaykh Muzaffer Ozak Al-Jerrahi leading the *hadra*

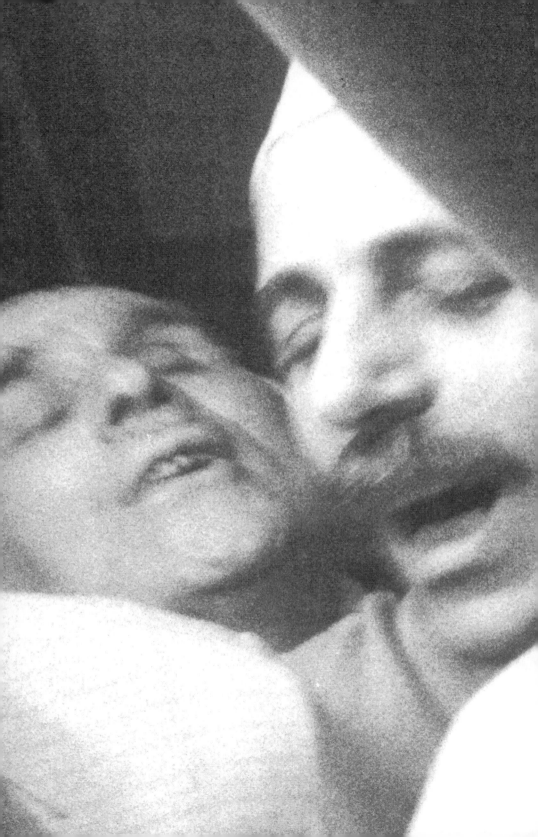

TO DANCE OR NOT TO DANCE

We were invited into the bourgeois home of a wealthy Saudi industrialist who was a dogmatic *Salafi* that constantly condemned Sufism but who loved my teacher Sayyid Omar Abdullah. The industrialist was denouncing the practice of the sacred dance (*hadra*) as a forbidden innovation (*bid'ah*) in Islam. When the industrialist left the salon where we were sitting Sayyid Omar jumped up mischievously and said to us *sotto voce*, "Now, if I stand here before you and declare God's Name, "*Allah!*"; is this forbidden?" We looked at him, shrugged and shook our heads. He then moved casually from one foot to another and said, "If I do this and say "*Allah!*" am I doing something forbidden?" Of course not. He then moved from one foot to another with more rhythm and said, "If I do this and say "*Allah! Allah!*" is this forbidden?" We shook our heads. Then he started to swirl around the floor with an imaginary partner and said, "But if I do this" and he began singing, 'Everybody loves Saturday Night! Everybody loves Saturday Night!' "Well, that is forbidden." What he was telling us is that what differentiates what is forbidden from what is permissible is the purpose and this is the classical Sufi approach to remembrance in all its various forms. When the industrialist returned Sayyid Omar sat down with an impish smile and continued to charm his unwitting host. And Sayyid Omar never practiced the *hadra* - except once.

During the post-colonial period in the 1960s when African states achieved their independence, Muslims across the continent were being marginalized because they had fallen behind Christians, Marxists and nationalists by rejecting secular education in favor of the traditional Islamic schools (*kuttab madaris*), which focused on memorizing the Qur'an and religious teaching. Delegations had been sent around Africa to try to convince Muslim parents to allow their children to have a more rounded secular education with little success.

One of the Muslim communities most resistant to change was in

Photo left: Shaykh Sefer Effendi and another dervish absorbed in *hadra* what was then the Belgian Congo. As one of Africa's pre-eminent educators, Sayyid Omar was sent on a tour to make yet another plea for secular education. In the Congo his presentation was to take place in the grand mosque after the Friday prayers. Sayyid Omar was the honored guest of the day. When the prayers were completed, he expected to stand up and make his speech. Instead, the whole congregation stood up and started a huge African-style *hadra*, which was absolutely wild. Although Sayyid Omar was a scholar and his Sufi practice did not include performance of the *hadra*, he joined the dance. He became so involved in the invocation that he was pushed into the center of the huge circle. He threw himself into this unfamiliar ritual heart and soul and led the community in the sacred dance. Then he was called on to give his talk. Up to that point none of the educators who had advocated secular education had any credibility, but now, as a leader of their *hadra*, Sayyid Omar was one of them. The whole community agreed to enter their children into the secular school system.

The *hadra*, which literally means "presence", is a galvanic practice among the Sufis of North Africa and the Levant, particularly those from the Qadiriyya-Shadhiliyya-Darqawiyya tradition, but also the Helveti of Turkey and other Sufi orders. It induces intense concentration, which is its purpose, and can, in the right circumstance, propel individuals into transcendent states (*ahwal*) and spiritual ecstasies (*jadhb* or *wajd*). In all authentic traditions there is a strict *adab*, or spiritual courtesy, demanded of those who perform *hadra*. It is almost always preceded by a long interval during which Sufi *qasa'id* are sung. *Qasa'id* are teaching odes on the sacred sciences, which encourage reflection and can lead to contemplation and deep spiritual states. The singing of the *diwans* of the saints prepares the heart for the intensity of the dance itself, which is accompanied by soaring voices singing *qasa'id*. When the *hadra* is completed, participants sit and listen to the recitation of the Qur'an, which is obligatory. The Qur'an returns the assembly to the Words of God, the supreme form of invocation. The recitation of Qur'an is followed by a discourse delivered by a man of knowledge. The *hadra* cleans and empties the hearts of the assembly and the discourse fills the empty vessels with knowledge, grounding those who may have been transported beyond the physical world, or, at times, triggering transcendent reflective states.

The 18th century Moroccan Shaykh Ahmed Ibn Ajiba, may God be well pleased with him, wrote:

"The category of dancing which is recommended is the dancing of the Sufis, the people of taste and state, whether they are in ecstasy or seeking ecstasy, whether that is in the presence of the *dhikr*, or in *sama'* (literally "hearing"). There is no doubt that the cure of the heart of forgetfulness and gathering with Allah is sought by whatever means there are..."

I had always been ambivalent about the *hadra*. On the one hand, I found the practice incredibly powerful, invigorating and at times intoxicating. On the other hand, it seemed to me to be a kind of crutch or shortcut that could easily be abused. I observed that those who focused on *hadra* over knowledge fell away from the true Path. As a novice I was exposed to *hadra* in its purest and most rigorous form, as part of a comprehensive process of purification that included study, contemplation, purification and spiritual companionship (*suhba*). From this vantage point there were other Sufi orders that focused their practice almost exclusively on the *hadra*, which seemed debased to me and I avoided their gatherings.

Although the Darqawi Sufi Order celebrated the *hadra*, and I enjoyed taking part to a certain extent, often as a singer, I was never altogether comfortable and always wondered whether it was essential. Si Fudul Al-Hawari Al-Sufi, the great Fesi scholar, was an active participant in the *hadra* and yet he was one of the most sober and grounded men I have ever met. So I asked him, point blank, if *hadra* was a necessary practice on the Path.

To my surprise, he said that it was not.

Many of the great *awliya* I have met refrained from openly commenting on the practice and authenticity of other contemporary Sufis, but Si Fudul demanded the highest standards of practice among those claiming spiritual transmission. I visited him once with a young Fesi disciple of a popular but unorthodox shaykh who attracted many disciples by promoting the spontaneous and uncontrolled practice of the *hadra*, which was dramatic, exciting and seductive to young people but which breached traditional *adab*. When the young man introduced himself as the disciple of this shaykh, Si Fudul shook his head and warned him sternly that his shaykh's practice was wrong and dangerous. The young man protested, obviously thinking of Si Fudul as old school. This exchange gave rise to palpable tension in the room. Neither man backed down. It was the only time I have ever seen this kind of encounter.

Although the *hadra* is not an essential practice in Sufism, it has become in some orders one of the most effective ways of keeping acolytes on the path.

Thursday Night Fever

In Egypt, my close friend Abdallah Schleifer dragged me to a weekly gathering led by an illustrious shaykh of the Burhaniyya Sufi Order. Shaykh Gamal ministered to thousands of Egyptians, Nubians and Sudanese and led a weekly *hadra* at his *zawiya* across from the Mosque of Sayyidina Husayn in the Azhar District of Cairo. Abdallah loved these gatherings but I avoided them. One night he insisted that I accompany him and I'm glad he did for I had something of a revelation. We arrived late, after the *dhikr* had begun. Hundreds of men were crushed together in the *zawiyya*, singing with gusto from the *diwans*. Shaykh Gamal spotted Abdallah, who was a regular, and made a place for us beside him. The room was ringing with the sound of *dhikr*. The invocation was loud and raucous, like the streets of Egypt. The *hadra* began. It was wild, a little scary and not at all to my taste.

It was a little like Saturday Night Fever...on Thursday. I wanted to get out but I was trapped in the horde of flailing bodies. Yet, slowly it dawned on me that these were men who might otherwise be playing *trictrac* and smoking *shisha* (hubbly bubbly) in some neighborhood *qahwa* (coffee house), or watching a soap opera, or worse. Instead they were remembering God. The *hadra* was a catalyst to keep them in remembrance, to seek *Allah* "by whatever means there are..."

"Movement during remembrance is a good thing because it brings energy to the body for the act of worship."

Shaykh Abdul Qadir Isa*

* Realities of Sufism, translated by Shuraqah Abdul Aziz.

SERENADE

When I was young the most arresting Sufi singers were from Algeria. The Algerians brought with them a distinctive pulsating rhythm to the Andalusian tradition of song that never failed to electrify their listeners. A delegation of Algerians would come to Morocco to celebrate the *Moussem* of Ibn Al-Habib. This was before the borders were closed between the two countries with the onset of the Polisario War between Morocco and Algeria.

The lead singer of the Algerian *fuqara* was a stout, cherubic gentleman with shining eyes behind thick spectacles. Hajj Omar hailed from the town of Boufarik, inland and south of Algiers. I first met him in Morocco at the *Moussem* of Ibn Al-Habib and then later in England when he came to visit.

Years later he came to Makkah and we spent time together. As I recall he was staying near Masjid Jinn, about two kilometers from the Holy Mosque. I picked him and his companion up from their hotel to take them into Jeddah. His friend had to mail a letter at the post office so we let him off and waited for him. Hajj Omar was sitting beside me. We waited silently. Suddenly, he turned toward me, leaned into my ear and began to sing. He sang intoxicating verses in a lilting rhythmic flow. His eyes glowed. He could make the heart dance with his voice. It was a moment of pure felicity.

**"All men are sure that I am in love,
But they know not whom I love.
There is in Man no beauty
That is not surpassed in beauty by a beautiful voice."**

**A verse chanted to Ibrahim Khawwas
sending him into ecstasy***

* related by Ali bin Uthman Al-Hujwiri in *Kashf Al-Mahjub, translated by Reynold Nicholson.*

THE HEART SHATTERER

He pierced the heart. When he sang, believers would weep. His voice was almost operatic in its power. I never knew his name. He was called "The Heart Shatterer" for his preternatural gift. He was an otherwise unremarkable man who lived in the city of Meknes. He was silenced suddenly; murdered in his sleep, his throat slit. A celestial gate slammed shut with brute force. God bless him.

"Cry, lover-nightengale. This is the place for it."

Khwaja Shems ud-Din Mohamed Hafiz-i Shirazi*

*The Diwan of Hafiz (The Green Sea of Heaven), translated by Elizabeth T. Gray Jr.

THE LIVING

**"The likeness of he who remembers God
and he who does not remember God
is like that of the living and the dead."**

The Prophet Mohamed*

**"Think ye I am this corpse ye are to bury?
I swear by God, this dead one is not I.
I in the Spirit am, and this my body
My dwelling was, my garment for a time.
I am a treasure: hidden I was beneath
This talisman of dust, wherein I suffered.
I am a pearl; a shell imprisoned me,
But leaving it, all trials I have left.
I am a bird, and this was once my cage;
But I have flown, leaving it as a token.
I praise God who hath set me free, and made
For me a dwelling in the heavenly heights.
Ere now I was a dead man in your midst,
But I have come to life, and doffed my shroud."**

Abu Hamid Al-Ghazali**

*Abu Musa Al-Ashari, *Sahih Al-Bukhari.*
** Said to have been found under a pillow after his death, translated by Martin Lings
Photo left: The grave marker of Habib Ahmad Mashhur Al Hadad in Al Maala in Makkah

175

DIRECT FROM PARADISE

When Shaykh Mohamed ibn Al-Habib lay on his deathbed, Si Hamid, his disciple, sat in an adjoining room, beside himself with grief. He was a gifted *qari* (one who recites the Qur'an) with a celestial voice and had been raised by the Shaykh from the time he was a small boy. He silently wept at the loss of his spiritual father, who was 100 years old. In his grief, he said to himself, "He is going to die. What will I do when he dies? I can't live without him." The moment this thought passed through his heart, the voice of his Shaykh rang out. "Si Hamid, come here!" Si Hamid rushed to the bedside of his Shaykh. Ibn Al-Habib sat up and admonished the young man. "Si Hamid, you must never think that! We do not die. The people of remembrance (*dhikr*) do not die. And the people of forgetfulness (*ghaflah*) are already dead!"

I never met Shaykh Mohamed ibn Al-Habib during his life but I met him in three vivid dreams. During my first visit to Meknes, the year after his passing, I was in a state of profound shock. I had never encountered men who had no interest in the ego, or, for that matter, in the world. Over an intense three-week period my hair began to turn gray. I was only 23 at the time. I was overwhelmed with the intensity of the practice of remembrance. My self-esteem plummeted. My heart became turbulent. In reaction I retreated into sleep. My friend Peter Sanders gave a slide show of the visit a month or two later. As a joke, almost every other shot in the sequence was a photo of me sleeping, much to the mirth of his audience.

Although I was embarrassed at the time, later on I discovered that retreating into sleep was the right thing to do, when I read the words of Moulay Al-Arabi ad-Darqawi:

"Have no fear of psychic suggestions when they assail you and flood your heart in waves ceaselessly renewed, but inwardly abandon all will to God and remain calm; do not be agitated, relax and do not be tense; and sleep, if you can, until you have your fill of it, for sleep is beneficial in times of distress; it brings marvelous benefits, for it is in itself abandonment to the divine will."

The author in an escapist slumber circa 1973

During one of these escapist slumbers, I had a dream that I was in the *zawiya* of Ibn Al-Habib at the far side of the large room, near the passageway leading to the apartments of the Shaykh's widows. The atmosphere was suffused with golden light and everything in the *zawiya* seemed to be made of gold. From the tomb, the Shaykh emerged and walked toward me. He was young and erect, not aged. Years later I saw a photo of Ibn Al-Habib as a young man and this was exactly the figure that walked toward me. His disciples were scattered along his path, prostrate before him. The atmosphere was majestic and powerful.

Many months later in England I had a second dream, one of the most vivid of my life. I had been feeling spiritually inadequate and, in spite of my conversion to Islam, felt that I remained in many respects an unbeliever. In the dream I was in Paradise, sitting in a room rich with carpets (*zarabiy mabthutha*) before Ibn Al-Habib. He was extremely beautiful, his skin light and luminous, his presence emanating tranquility. He spoke to me in a beautiful voice, in rhymed couplets in ravishing classical Arabic. I didn't speak a word of Arabic at the time, but clearly understood every word he said. I can't remember the exact words but the gist of his poem was, "Do not worry. Even I was afflicted with *kufr* (unbelief)."

This was a puzzling, not to say troubling, statement. I shared the dream with another, more experienced *faqir* who was disturbed. He said, "No this is wrong. This can't be a true dream." I only understood the meaning of the dream years later upon reading a statement by Ibn Al-Arabi referring to *kufr* in its etymological sense as the act of covering or hiding something, meaning that only the Gnostics (*Arifin*) were completely free from unbelief when the veils had been lifted, their hearts uncovered and the illumination of Truth revealed. Much later I came across an extraordinary passage from the *Maqalat* of Shems-i Tabrizi, the spiritual master of Maulana Jalalud'din Rumi:

"In my view, no one can become a Muslim just once. He becomes a Muslim, then he becomes an unbeliever, then again he becomes a Muslim, and each time something comes out of him. So it goes until he becomes perfect."*

Indeed, this was the meaning of my dream and the words of comfort from my shaykh direct from Paradise.

I had a third dream of Ibn Al-Habib. In it he counseled me on

* The Autobiography of Shems-i-Tabriz, translated by William C. Chittick.

weeping. "Turn your tears inward," he said. "Let your tears water your heart so that it will be nourished."

I passed before the tomb of the Messenger of God for the first time and stepped away from the procession of visitors being herded by the *Salafi* guards stationed before the cast brass grill to prevent any open demonstrations of love for the Prophet. This was in 1980 and at this point their traffic control was less intrusive than it eventually became. I sat unobtrusively with my back to the *qibla* facing the tomb. And I silently recited the Prayer on the Prophet, peace be upon him, revealed by the Messenger of God to Shaykh Mohamed ibn Al-Habib, may God be well pleased with him, as he sat many years before not far from where I was sitting:

"Oh God, send blessings and salutations through all Your Perfections and in all Your Revelations to our Master and Guardian Mohamed, First of the Lights overflowing from the Seas of the Majesty of the Essence, the one who realizes in both the inward and outward domains, the meanings of the Names and Qualities. He is the first of those to praise and worship through all the modes of worship and means of approach, the one who helps all that exists in the Two Worlds of spirit and form, and upon his family and companions, which unveil to us his noble face, both in dream visions and awake. And bestow upon us direct knowledge of You and of him at every level of the Way and every realm of Your presence. And we ask You, O our Guardian and Protector, by his honor, that Your Infinite Kindness be ever with us in our movement and rest, our glances and thoughts."

I repeated this prayer again and again, as a parade of worshippers passed before me, longing for intimacy, longing to be included in the presence of the Messenger.

I sat, back to *qibla*, trying not to attract the attention of the *Salafi* sentries upbraiding worshippers for any emotional displays, moving the crowds swiftly past the brass grill. I silently repeated Ibn Al-Habib's blessing on the Prophet, hands raised in supplication, knocking at an invisible door, longing for one undeserved salutation from our Messenger, peace and blessings be upon him, who was so close, yet so far from me. Gradually, a hand of light reached inside of me. The flood gates opened. My heart overflowed. Tears spilled. I felt as if the Messenger had touched my heart, my salutation was returned. I bowed my head, covered my eyes with one hand and watered my heart with tears from the salutation of the Prophet Mohamed, may God bless him and give him peace, through the sacred blessing revealed to Shaykh Mohamed ibn Al-Habib, may God be pleased with him.

I lived for a time in the attic of a brown shingle house in Berkley, California and celebrated one Ramadan there. During the month of fasting I prayed behind the Messenger of God in my dream. I did not see his face, peace be upon him. I could only see the back of his head and his black cloak. Many years later I asked my shaykh Sayyid Omar Abdullah, may God be well pleased with him, the meaning of the dream. He said, "It means that you are trying to follow the *Sunna* of the Messenger."

"He who has seen me in a dream has seen me in reality for the devil cannot take my form."

The Prophet Mohamed*

---

* Reported by Abu Huraira in *Sahih Al-Bukhari* and *Sahih Muslim*.

IN TRANSIT

In 1976 I was on my way to Cairo from London. I was to change planes in Damascus for the connection to Cairo. When we landed at dawn, I grabbed my bag and went to the transit desk. The Syrian Air ground staffer looked at my ticket and told me that I had no reservation for the flight to Cairo and that the flight was full. I told him I had to get on the flight. He said it was impossible. I asked when the next flight would be. He told me it was in five days. Five days?! "I can't wait here for five days! I have to get on the flight tonight. Who can I talk to?" He told me I would have to go to the ticket office in Damascus.

I caught a taxi into town with a Jordanian girl who had been studying abroad and who was on her way to Amman for the holidays. There had been another upheaval in the Arab-Israeli conflict and the city was filled with Palestinian refugees. Hotels were full. With the help of my taxi-mate, I managed to find a cheap hotel in town where I left my bags and set off to find the Syrian Air office. It was early morning and it was Ramadan. The streets were empty except for a few soldiers and students who all seemed to be in military uniform.

When I arrived at the Syrian Air office it was still closed but a long line was already forming. I took my place in the queue. When the doors opened I went to a desk manned by an expressionless young woman. I explained that I had a ticket with a reservation to Cairo that had not been confirmed and that I had to get the connecting flight this evening. She looked at me impassively and pointed across the room to another desk. I walked over and repeated my story. He listened and directed me across the room to another desk. I walked over, waited in line and then repeated my story. I was directed to another desk. And so it went until I had been sent full circle back to the expressionless young woman. I said, "Excuse me but where can I find the manager?"

Silently, she pointed to a desk at the corner of the room surrounded by people yelling at a harried mustachioed fellow who was engaged in an intense discussion with one of several agitated customers.

I waited at the back of the circle and while this animated interchange was going on I tapped the man in front of me on the shoulder. He looked around. I said quietly, "Excuse me, do you speak English?" He said he did, so I asked him if he could do me a favor and explain my predicament, which I retold for about the tenth time. He was very polite and when there was a momentary lull in the heated exchange, he caught the attention of the manager who looked around exasperated, saying, "hah?" (translation: "what do you want?"). My interlocutor quickly explained my situation to the manager who listened intently. He then barked out a brief response and returned to the defense of his realm against a phalanx of frustrated customers. I eagerly asked my kind representative what he had said. He turned to me ruefully. "He said... he doesn't want to know."

I left the Syrian Air office with the grim prospect of staying in a fleabag hotel in a conflict zone for five long days in Ramadan without knowing a soul. I had days to kill so I decided to visit the tomb of Shaykh Al-Akbar, Muhyid'din ibn Al-'Arabi, the Seal of the Saints, may God be well pleased with him. His tomb was on a hill above the city. I walked up the hill until I found the mosque. After making two cycles of prayer greeting the mosque and reading from the Qur'an, I repaired to the tomb of Ibn Al-'Arabi. I recited *Sura Ikhlas*, prayed for the shaykh and asked God to help me on my way. I was fasting and exhausted from a long journey. I reclined by the tomb and fell into a deep, dreamless sleep. When I woke up I knew with a sense of calm certainty that I had to return to the airport. I prayed for Shaykh Al-Akbar and asked forgiveness for my wrong actions. I returned to the fleabag hotel, retrieved my suitcase and caught a taxi back to Damascus Airport. I went to the check-in desk with my unconfirmed ticket, was checked in without question and made the flight to Cairo.

Perhaps it would have happened anyway, but at the very least the serenity of the tomb of the Seal of the Saints gave me the clarity I needed to stay on course.

**"Travel not from creature to creature,
otherwise you will be like a donkey at the mill:
Roundabout he turns,
his goal the same as his departure.
Rather, go from creatures to the Creator."**

Ibn Ata'illah Al-Iskandari*

---

* *Al-Hikam*, translted by Victor Danner.

PERFUME

Shaykh Ibn Ata'illah Al-Iskandari, author of *Al-Hikam*, *Taj Al-Arus* and other seminal Sufi treatises, is one of the greatest Sufi saints in history. He is buried in the City of the Dead, the vast cemetery that stretches for miles along the Northern edge of Cairo embracing the tombs of some of the most illustrious saints and scholars of Islam, including Imam Shafi'i, Dhu'l Nun Al-Misr, Ibn Al-Farid, Muhammad Wafa, Ali Wafa, and many, many others. As with so many of the tombs in this awesome burial ground, Ibn Ata'illah's grave site had deteriorated almost to the point of being lost. There was a broken down marker in the general area where the saint was supposed to be buried but no indication of an actual tomb.

During his tenure as Shaykh Al-Azhar, Dr. Abdul Halim Mahmoud, may God be well-pleased with him, dispatched a search party to the general area where the Shaykh was interred to try to re-locate the exact grave site and erect a proper memorial for the great saint. The area was a scene of total desolation, forgotten and neglected for many decades, if not centuries. The group spread out and began sifting through the rubble and ruins without success until, suddenly they caught the scent of a unique, unworldly fragrance. They followed the perfume until it was overpowering and began to clear the stones and debris and dug down until they found the body of Ibn Ata'illah Al-Iskandari perfectly preserved, as if he were asleep, wreathed in an intoxicating celestial perfume.

Abdel Halim Magahed was a wealthy merchant who had made his fortune selling construction machinery. As a pious Muslim, he decided that the time had come for him to build a mosque. Many Muslims who attain wealth in life aspire to build a mosque in response to the Prophetic recommendation.

Abdel Halim Megahed was not a Sufi. In fact, he was a *Salafi* who was against the practice of Sufism. But he had a business acquaintance that encouraged him to consult with the Shaykh of Al-Azhar before deciding on where to build his mosque. When they met, Shaykh Al-Azhar immediately recommended that the businessman build a mosque beside the newly re-discovered tomb of Ibn Ata'illah. Abdel Halim came away from the meeting with profound misgivings and went back to his *Salafi* friends who talked him out of building a mosque beside the tomb of a Sufi.

Then he had a vivid dream. In the dream he was standing before the famous Mosque of Abul Abbas Al-Mursi in Alexandria. Abul Abbas Al-Mursi, the heir of Imam Al-Shadhili, was Ibn Ata'illah's spiritual master and predecessor. In the dream Shaykh Abul Abbas was standing in front of the mosque and holding the hand of Shaykh Ibn Ata'illah. He addressed Abdel Halim, saying, "They have built this mosque for me. I would like for you to build a mosque for my brother." Abdel Halim reported this dream to Shaykh Al-Azhar, who was delighted. He said, "This means you must build this mosque."

Despite his qualms Abdel Halim proceeded with design and construction. He put all the funds required to build the mosque into a safe in his office. Before construction began he withdrew a large sum of money from the safe to pay the first installment to his contractors, recording his sums in a ledger. The first phase of building commenced. When the time came for him to pay the second installment Abdel Halim opened his safe to withdraw the funds and found that he had exactly the same amount of money he had before he made the first withdrawal. At first he assumed that he had made an accounting error. When he returned the next month to withdraw the third installment again the same amount of money was in the safe as before the beginning of the project.

Abdel Halim began to worry that he might be losing his mind. He thought that perhaps the *Salafis* who warned him about building a mosque near a tomb had been right. He went to Shaykh Al Azhar in a state of high anxiety and told him what was happening. Shaykh Al-Azhar beamed ecstatically and told him that this was from the blessing of Shaykh Ibn Ata'illah. "If you had kept this miracle to yourself, it would have continued until the mosque was completed," the Shaykh said. "Now that you have shared this, you'll have to use your funds." And this is what happened.

When I first lived in Egypt during the 1970s, just after the completion of the Mosque of Ibn Ata'illah, I came to know Abdul Halim Megahed. My wife was pregnant at the time with our first child. As young first time parents we were both apprehensive. Before leaving Egypt I visited him in his office in Bab Al Luk and mentioned this to him. Abdul Halim gave me a talisman for my wife to read during her labor. She did and found that when she gazed at the talisman during her contractions her birth pains disappeared.

The mosque of Ibn Ata'illah Al-Iskandari is a magnet for wayfarers today and I pray that Abdel Halim, may God have Mercy on him, is resting peacefully in his house in Paradise.

"If anyone builds a mosque for God, God will build a house for him in Paradise."

The Prophet Mohamed*

* Sahih Al-Bukhari and Sahih Muslim.

TRANSFIGURED NIGHT

I led a group of about ten Sufi novices on horseback and donkey from the Moroccan city of Larache into the Rif Mountains toward the tomb of Moulay Abdul Salaam bin Mashish, the spiritual master of Imam Abul Hassan Al-Shadhili, may God be well pleased with them. In Morocco visiting the tomb of this great saint was called "The Pilgrimage of the Poor" (*Hajj Al-Fuqara*) because the devout who couldn't afford to make the Hajj would make a visitation (*ziyara*) to Jabal Alam, the mountain of Moulay Abdul Salam.

Moulay Abdul Salam ibn Mashish was born in the village of Aghyul in either 1146 or 1148 AD. His father Moulay Slimane Mashish was a descendent of the Prophet Mohamed, may God bless him and give him peace, and a great saint who is buried beside the Mashishiya *Zawiya* across the valley from his son's haunting primordial tomb on the high tor. It was said that by the age of seven Moulay Abdul Salam had become utterly God intoxicated (*majdhoub*). He studied the religious sciences in Northern Morocco, settled in Ceuta to teach children the Qur'an and joined the Almohad army in Andalucía before withdrawing from the world to a cave in Jabal Alam to spend the last twenty years of his life in remembrance and contemplation.

Abul Hassan Al-Shadhili traveled across the world to meet Ibn Mashish and became his only disciple.

"When I drew near him, he was living in Ghumara in a lodge on the top of a mountain. I bathed at a spring by the base of that mountain, forsook all dependence on my own knowledge and works, and went up toward him as one in need. Just then he was coming down toward me, wearing a patched cloak, and on his head a cap of palm leaves. 'Welcome to 'Ali ibn 'Abd Allah ibn 'Abd Al-Jabbar,' he said to me, 'O, 'Ali, you have come up to us destitute of your knowledge and works, so you will receive from us the riches of this world and the next.'

"Awe of him seized me. So I remained with him for some days until God awakened my perception, and I saw that he possessed many supernatural powers (*kharq al-'adat*)."

This fabled meeting produced one of the most powerful and enduring Sufi traditions in the world. The Shadhiliya Order and its many branches extend across North Africa and throughout the Middle East and to Asia. At the age of 63, Ibn Mashish was murdered by Ibn Abi Al-Tawajin and is buried on the mountain-top, above the cave in the cliff face that was his home.

We rode up the winding pathways to the summit of Jabal Alam retracing the steps of Imam Shadhili. We drank from 'Ayn Al-Shadhili, the spring that burst forth from beneath the saintly wayfarer's feet so that he could make the ritual ablution before approaching his spiritual master. As we came closer to the pla-teau, the mountain became increasingly verdant. Springs flowed from the mountain sides.

When we reached the summit in late afternoon, young Berber children ran to greet us. At first I thought that this was moun-tain hospitality until I felt their hands. They were cold, stiff, outstretched, mendicant hands. These young children had the faces of hardened beggars looking for small change. It was jar-ring. We tethered our animals and spread out across the open-air mosque which extended across the plateau from the ancient whitewashed tomb.

A floor of smooth white cork tiles surrounded a primitive white mud brick structure built around an ancient, gnarled oak tree with bare sagging branches marking the burial site of the saint. The cork floor extended out from the tomb toward the direction of prayer (*qibla*) which ended in a sheer precipice, dropping sud-denly into space, facing a vast panorama of the green gorge one thousand feet below with cultivated fields sweeping for miles to the rising peaks of the Rif range on the horizon.

After greeting the tomb and taking in the breathtaking view, we repaired to a primitive mosque – nothing more than a plain white room with straw matting – set at a short distance from the grave site, and prayed the sunset prayer. After the prayer the Imam began making supplication in exchange for money. It was like selling indulgences. Members of the assembly would hand him cash and he would pray for them. I had never seen anything like it in my life. I was told that this was a mountain Berber custom. Custom or not, I found the practice repellent and led my group outside into the cold evening air.

It was the night of *Mawlid An-Nabi* – the birth of the Prophet Mohamed, may God give him peace. We formed a circle and began reciting prayers on the Prophet, including the famous prayer of Ibn Mashish:

"First! O Last! O Manifest! O Most Hidden! Hear my call as You heard the call of your servant Zakariyya and grant me victory through You, for You and support me through You, for You, and join me to You and come between myself and anything other than You..."

By the time we disbanded, each to our own private devotions, night had fallen. An immense white moon high in the crystal sky radiated an ethereal canopy of light above the Rif Valley. In the bracing icy air I walked across the white cork floor, glowing in moon-wash, to the edge of the mosque. The floor ended abruptly – a sheer drop into the abyss. But the valley had filled with clouds to the very edge of the floor, creating a vast carpet illuminated by the piercing white moon, extending from the white mosque floor of Moulay Abdul Salam to the distant peaks at the far perimeter of the valley.

This dazzling nocturnal vision was Blakean in its sacred power. I fully expected ranks of angels to descend from the white heavens and was tempted to step out from the edge of the precipice onto the soft illusory cloud cover and walk across the sky. I lifted my hands in awe and *takbir*, looking out on the dreamlike spectacle before me – a sign on the horizon – and began a cycle of prayer that would take me to dawn on this white celestial night bathed in the living illuminated presence of the departed saint.

**"Firmly root us and support us
and subjugate to us this Sea
As You subjugated the Sea to Moses
And You subjugated the Fire to Abraham
And You subjugated the Mountains
and the Iron to David
And you subjugated the Wind
and the Demons and Jinn to Solomon.
So subjugate to us every Sea of Yours
on the Earth, in the Skies,
the Dominion and the Celestial Kingdom
And the Sea of this World
and the Sea of the World to come..."**

Shaykh Abu'l Hassan Al Shadhili*

* Orison of the Sea (*Hizb Al-Bahr*), translated by Nurad-din Durkee.

EPILOGUE

"God brings every stranger back to his homeland."

Moulay Al 'Arabi Ad-Darqawi*

*   Letters of a Sufi Master: The Shaykh Ad-Darqawi, translated by Titus Burkhardt

FULL CIRCLE

orty years have passed since I began this path. My guides have gone. I've been alone, holding to the rope of remembrance, keeping company when I can with like-minded seekers, clinging to the memories of saints, hoping for God's Forgiveness and Mercy and secretly longing for illumination in spite of all my many shortcomings and wrong actions.

I wrote this book to remind myself of the gifts I've received along the Way and to nurture the love for the men of God that have crossed my path and touched my heart. In the process of gathering my thoughts and recording my memories I've been reminded of my weakness and my need. As I have aged, the aspirations that seemed so remote and unreachable in my youth now seem like near imperatives. As life quickens and rolls up like a scroll, the world has lost its pull. The act of remembrance has become my anchor and my solace and as love for the world has faded within me, the need for proximity, illumination and an opening has taken hold of my heart.

When Shaykh Mohamed ibn Al-Habib died at the age of 100 in 1972 he left no successor. The great saints of the order, his obvious heirs, had all refused acclamation, and the pretenders – the men of false claims – were exposed and rejected. I'd been initiated into the Habibiyya immediately after the death of Ibn Al-Habib and spent my first years as a novice in the occasional company of his great disciples in Morocco but without the guidance of a living Shaykh of Instruction. Indeed, I really had no idea what the relation between spiritual master and disciple was like until I reached Makkah Al-Mukarramah, sat with great masters of the Way and found my shaykhs in Sayyid Omar Abdullah and Habib Ahmad Mashhur Al-Haddad. When they passed away, I felt cut adrift, clinging to the wisdom and practice they imparted to me, like a life preserver or a fragment of wreckage that could keep me afloat.

Years ago I was relieved to learn that Moulay Hashem Balghiti had emerged, after a 25 year gap, as the living Shaykh of the Habibiyya Order. Long ago we'd been told by the saint Sidi Mohamed Sahrawi, that Moulay Hashem was a hidden saint. This was an astonishing revelation for at the time he displayed no outward signs of sainthood. His acclamation as heir to Ibn Al-Habib had been confirmed by the greatest living saints of the Habibiyya Order, including Si Fudul Al-Hawari and Sidi Mohamed Bil Kurshi.

I was living at the far end of the Middle East at the time and still engaged in the practice of my shaykhs. Writing this book became the catalyst that propelled me to Morocco and the company of Moulay Hashem.

It had been a quarter century since I'd last visited Meknes. I arrived in Morocco on *Eid Al-Adha* and on the third day of the *Eid* made my way to Meknes. I didn't quite know what to expect. I remembered Moulay Hashem well from my time as a novice 40 years ago. He was an elegant, affluent young businessman, the son of a great Sufi saint, who was tremendously generous and who hosted many nights of invocation in his beautiful home.

Moulay Hashem's son and deputy (*muqaddam*) Moulay Abdul Kabir met us in the center of Meknes and guided us to his father's home. My companions and I were ushered into a long rectangular room (*iwan*) off the main closed multi-storied atrium courtyard in his large traditional town house.

To describe Moulay Hashem as understated would be something of an understatement. He was disarmingly unceremonious and self-effacing. He seemed the embodiment of the statement of Dhu'l Nun Al-Misri:

"The Gnostic (*Arif*) is more lowly every day, because he is approaching nearer to his Lord every moment."*

I felt instantly at ease in his company, as if I'd always known him and was just dropping by casually for lunch. He served us delicious, perfectly prepared lamb. Although we had intended to find a hotel, once we were inside the house, there was no question but that we would stay with him. Everything about him was completely natural and relaxed.

After lunch I came right to the point. I explained that I'd been on the Path for 40 years, first as a disciple of Ibn Al-Habib and later under the guidance of Al-Haddad who had passed away many years before. "I'm on my own now. I've reached a point in my life where I've lost all interest in the world. The only thing I want to do is to remember God, overcome my passions and attain real knowledge and illumination." After saying this I expected to be let down gently – to be told to lower my expectations, that I had a long and difficult road ahead of me. Instead, when I finished, he leaned forward, smiled, looked me straight in the eye and said one word: "*Sahel*" ("It's easy").

And I knew, for the first time in my life, that he was right, that in spite of everything, the goal was within reach.

We prayed together, recited the glorious litany of Ibn Al-Habib together and ate together. Moulay Hashem said, "It is through the prayer on the Prophet Mohamed, peace be upon him, and love of the Prophet that you receive knowledge and an Opening." He admonished us to balance the invocation of the Great

---

* From *Kashf Al-Mahjub*, translated by Reynold A. Nicholson

Name ("*Allah*") with Prayer on the Prophet (*Salat An-Nabi*). "The Name of God is hot," he said. "The Prayer on the Prophet cools the heart."

He said, "Do what you like, but you will regret every hour that you have not remembered God."

He told us that at the beginning of the path the master holds the disciple like a baby close to his heart, protecting him. Then, when he has matured and is ready, the master turns him away toward the Light of God, and an Opening.

I realized that all the years I was with my two shaykhs, Sayyid Omar Abdullah and Habib Ahmed Mashhur Al-Haddad, that I was like a baby in their arms, that they were holding me close, protecting me as I raised my family and made my way in the world. Now I yearned for the Opening.

He spoke of the relationship between master and disciple. He said that the master cannot take a disciple unless he recognizes him; that is, he has known him in the unseen, from before Time. After he said this, he fell silent.

I leaned toward the shaykh, smiled and said, "Let me ask you something. *Do you recognize me?*" He laughed and said, "That depends on you." I laughed and was about to say, "That's not fair, you can't turn the tables on me after saying what you just said," but before I had the chance, he said to me, "Are you ready?"

"Yes."

He motioned me to sit beside him. When he took my hand and began a recitation for me to repeat, I disappeared.

When I returned I wept.

I had come full circle. I had come home.

"To the extent that the disciple snuffs himself out in the shaykh, he disappears into the true God."

Shaykh Ahmad ibn 'Ajiba*

* From the Autobiography (*Fahrasa*), translated by Jean Louis Michon.

ABOUT THE AUTHOR

Michael Sugich is a native of Santa Barbara, California and studied at UCLA and the California Institute of the Arts. He was initiated into a traditional Sufi order in 1972. Since that time he has studied Sufi doctrine and practice with spiritual masters across the Arab and Islamic world. He lived for 23 years in the precincts of the sacred city of Makkah Al Mukarama where he kept company with many men of knowledge and illumination. His Muslim name is Haroon.

Above: The author with Moulay Hashem Balghiti

GLOSSARY

A Note on Terms

Although I have tried to make the language and references as accessible and easy to understand as possible, there are necessarily some technical terms that require explanation.

Allah: God

I have used the Name Allah and God interchangeably in the text. For the purposes of this exposition, there is no difference whatsoever.

Arifbillah or **Arif**: Knower of God or Knower; most commonly translated as Gnostic. The *Arifbillah* is the possessor of direct knowledge of God.

Awtad (*singular* **Watad**): Literally Pillars. In Sufi metaphysics, the *Awtad* are four living masters, who, in the unseen, preserve the spiritual order, including the *Qutb* or Pole of the Universe who is the spiritual representative of the Prophet Mohamed, peace and blessings be upon him.

Baqabillah or **Baqa**: Literally, 'to remain with or subsist in God'. This is the supreme state of spiritual enlightenment where the slave has full awareness of duality, but sees phenomena as not other than God. The concept was first articulated by the 9th century Sufi master Abu Sa'id Al-Kharraz in Book of the Secret.

Bid'ah: Literally, "something new", an innovation in Islam that is not part of the *Sunna* of the Prophet Mohamed, peace be upon him. Scholars classify *bid'ah* in two categories: good innovation (*bid'ah hasanah*), which is harmonious with the Qur'an and Sunnah, and bad innovation (*bid'ah sayyi'ah*), which conflicts with the Qur'an and Sunnah.

Burnoose: A cloak.

Da'i: One who calls people to the Truth, to Islam, to the Path. A da'i is a communicator who should embody the message he delivers.

Dervish: The Persian term for a follower of the Sufi Path. The

Arabic name is most commonly *Faqir*, or poor man.

Dhikru'llah: Remembrance of God - the linchpin of all Sufi practice, indeed of all Muslim practice, is the act of remembrance or invocation of God (*dhikru'llah*). I would argue that the practice of invocation or remembrance is essential to all religious practice from Muslim, Christian, Jewish, Hindu and Buddhist traditions and the traditions of all true faiths. The recitation of the Qur'an, Bible, Torah, Vedas, Sutras, Upanishads and other sacred books is a form of remembrance. The Sufis consider recitation of the Qur'an the highest form of remembrance of God. In the Holy Qur'an there are many references to remembrance of God.

Diwan: a collection of odes, usually in rhymed couplets. Each ode is called a *qasida* (plural: *qasa'id*). In the Sufi tradition the diwan is composed by a teaching shaykh or spiritual master.

Djellaba: a traditional Moroccan robe. The Moroccan *djellaba* has a hood. The Egyptian robe, without a hood, is called a *gellabiyya*. In the Gulf countries the robe is called a *thobe*.

Dua'a: Supplication.

Eid: The feast or celebration marking the end of Ramadan, the month of fasting (*Eid Al-Fitr*), and the culmination of the annual Pilgrimmage (*Eid Al-Adha*).

Fanafillah (Fana): Literally annihilation in God. This is the goal of the seeker, when the self is obliterated in Divine light. Again, this doctrine was first articulated by Abu Sa'id Al-Kharraz (see *Baqabillah*).

Faqir (plural **Fuqara**): Literally a poor man (female, *faqira*) or, in plural, the poor. In Sufism faqir refers to a man on the Sufi Way in reference to the disciples having "renounced all things external and internal, and have turned entirely to [God]" . One of the Sufis explained that "the *faqir* is not he whose hand is empty of provisions, but he whose nature is empty of desires." In Eastern Sufism the word used is *Dervish*, or *Darwish*.

Ghusl: Full ritual ablution, performed after the act of sex or in preparation for a sacred act, such as the performance of *Hajj* or *Umrah*.

Hadra: Literally "Presence", this is an auditory practice that in Western Sufism takes the form of a dance where devotees invoke the Names of God, usually standing in a circle, hands joined, often swaying or moving to the rhythms of the invocation and the collective breath.

Haik: A traditional cloth head-cover worn in Northwest Africa over the turban (*'imamah*) and wrapped around the neck. The *haik* is similar to the *ghutra* or *shummagh* worn in the Arabian Gulf but worn differently.

Hajj: the Greater Pilgrimage to Makkah Al-Mukarramah, one of the Five Pillars of Islam.

Ihram: The two pieces of seamless white cloth prescribed for male pilgrims to wrap around their waists and cover their upper torso during the greater and lesser pilgrimages (*Hajj* and *'Umrah*).

Imara: Literally 'to fill up'. Another term used to refer to the sacred dance or *hadra* of the Sufis, particularly in North Africa.

Jadhb: Literally 'attraction', an ecstatic state where the worshipper is overwhelmed with the presence of God.

Janazah: Muslim funeral. *Salat Al-Janazah* is the Muslim funeral prayer, also called *Salat Al-Mawt* (prayer for the dead).

Ka'aba: The House of God, built by the Prophet Abraham and the epicenter of Islam. All Muslims pray toward the Ka'aba.

Kashf: Unveiling, literally raising of a curtain or veil. The term refers to an opening of spiritual intuition or insight.

Khalifa: Literally "one who stands in place of". In Sufism a *khalifa* is a designated representative of the shaykh.

Khalwa: Spiritual retreat.

Ksar: Literally a "castle" (classical Arabic: *qasr*). In North Africa a *ksar* is generally a fortified village or desert fort.

Laylat Al-Fuqara: Literally "Night of the Poor"; a gathering of Sufis for the remembrance of God.

Ma'arifa: Direct spiritual knowledge of God; gnosis.

Mabkhara (plural **Mabakhir**): Incense burner.

Majdhoub: One who is ecstatic, God-intoxicated, overwhelmed by *jadhb* (rapture) to the point of madness; sometimes described as a Holy Madman. When the great ancient Sufi Shibli was accused of being mad, he answered: "In your eyes I am mad and you are sane. May God increase me in my madness and increase you in your sanity!"

Majlis: Literally "Place of Sitting"; a gathering for remembrance or learning.

Mas'a: The track between the mounts of Safa and Marwa where Sayyida Hajar ran in search of water for her infant, the Prophet Isma'il, peace be upon them.

Mataf: The circular area around the Kaaba where pilgrims and worshippers perform the *Tawaf* or circumambulation of God's House.

Mawlid: Celebration of the birth of the Prophet Mohamed, peace be upon him.

Minza: A public traditional sitting area in an Arab house or *zawiya*, akin to a living room or salon.

Mu'adhin: One who calls worshippers to prayer (makes the adhan).

Muqaddam: An appointed deputy of a spiritual master. The *muqaddam* of a Sufi order is generally a more experienced disciple who has been assigned by the Shaykh to help guide disciples and administrate the practice. The title does not indicate spiritual knowledge.

Murid: The root meaning of this word relates to willpower and in Sufism refers to a disciple or follower of a Shaykh. In one sense the murid surrenders his will to the Shaykh. In another sense the murid exercises his will by taking the path to God.

Murshid: Literally, "one who guides", which in Sufism refers to a true spiritual master.

Mutawif: Literally one who makes *Tawaf* or circumambulation of the Kaaba but in common usage the word refers to one who guides pilgrims during the Hajj. This entails the organization of accommodation, food and transport during the pilgrimage. Originally the *mutawifeen* (plural of *mutawif*) were learned men who guided pilgrims from their home countries to Makkah and helped them perform the Hajj rituals. In Saudi Arabia the position became hereditary and commercial until the government restructured the *Mutawifeen* into organizations, serving specific countries and regions.

Pir: The Persian Sufi term for master or guide. The generic Arabic term would be Shaykh or *Murshid* (one who guides).

Qari: One who recites the Qur'an.

Qasida (plural **Qasa'id**): An ode, usually in rhymed couplets. Qasa'id have been written by great Sufi saints for the purpose of imparting wisdom teaching and spiritual knowledge and as a form of *dhikru'llah*. One of the earliest composers of *qasa'id* in the Islamic tradition was the Companion Hassan bin Thabit.

Qibla: Direction Muslims face in prayer toward the Holy Kaaba in Makkah Al Mukarramah.

Qutb: Literally the 'Pole' or 'Axis', and refers to a living saint who is the highest spiritual authority of his age and the axis of the unseen hierarchy of living saints. At times the Qutb is well known, as was the case with Shaykh Abu Madyan Al-Ghawth and Imam Abu'l Hassan Al-Shadhili, at other times the *Qutb* is hidden. The hidden *Qutb* of this time was revealed to the Shaykh Moulay Hashem Balghiti in an encounter at Moulay Idris Zerhoun.

Ru'ya: A true visionary dream.

Sadaqa: Alms.

Sa'ee: The seven circuits between the mounts of Safa and Marwa Muslims must walk as part of the 'Umrah to commemorate Hajaar's search for water. Literally Sa'ee means "effort".

Salaf: Those who believe that Muslims should return to the essential practice of the first Community at the time of the Prophet Mohamed, peace be upon him, and reject all other subsequent historical iterations of Islam. Many follow the teachings of Ibn Taymiyya and Mohamed ibn Abdul Wahhab. *Salafis* completely reject Shi'aa Islam and Sufism as innovation (*bida'a*). In the media *Salafis* are often described as fundamentalists or Islamists.

Sunni extremists who advocate violence claim to be *Salafis*. However, not all *Salafis* are extremists.

Salat Al-Mawt: Literally, prayer for the dead.

Shariah: Literally "The Road"; Islamic canonic law, based upon the Qur'an and Prophetic traditions.

Suhba: Spiritual companionship.

Sunna: The practice of the Prophet Mohamed, peace be upon him, based upon hadith literature.

Tasbih: A Muslim rosary, or prayer beads. Also called *Sibha*.

Talqin: In Islamic tradition *Talqin* is sitting at the side of a person's deathbed reciting with them the *kalimah tayyiba* (the *shahada*), and awakening hope and good expectation in the dying person's heart. In the terminology of *Tassawuf*, *talqin* is the formalized method of transmission of *awrad* and *adhkar*, usually with the recipient knee-to-knee, facing the transmitter and most often holding his hand.

Tarawih: Literally, "to rest", which refers to resting between every four cycles of prayer. *Salat Al-Tarawih* are prescribed superogatory prayers recited during Ramadan, after the night prayers.

Tariqa: Literally, "Path" or "Way". In Sufi terminology, a *tariqa* is a Sufi brotherhood or order, composed of disciples (*murideen*) who follow the teachings of a spiritual master (*murshid*), or *shaykh*. A Sufi *Tariqa* can be large, with thousands or even millions of followers, as in the Shadhili or Tijani orders, or smaller with dozens or hundreds of followers.

Tawaf: Circumambulation of seven circuits around the Holy Kaaba, a ritual practice for Muslims visiting the Holy Mosque in Makkah, tracing back to the time of Abraham, and forming an essential part of the Greater and Lesser Pilgrimages (*Hajj* and *Umrah*). The area surrounding the Ka'aba is called the *Mataf*, (literally, "the place of *Tawaf*").

Umrah: The Lesser Pilgrimage, wherein the Muslim dons the *ihram* and performs the *tawwaf* and *sa'ee*. *Umrah* is an integral part of the Hajj.

Wajd: Usually translated as ecstasy. Al-Hujwiri wrote, "*Wajd* is a mystery between the seeker and the Sought, which only revelation can expound."

Wali'ullah (plural **Awliya'ullah**): Literally, Friend of God, signifying a man of deep spiritual knowledge and attainment – a Saint. In Islam saints are not canonized as in the Christian tradition, but "recognized" by other gnostics. Some *Awliya'ullah* are completely hidden.

Wird (plural **Awrad**): A prescribed litany recited regularly. In explaining the wird in his book "Realities of Sufism", Shaykh Abdul Qadir 'Isa refers to the Arabic lexicon al-Misbah, which defines a *wird* as: "A daily regimen of reading...The Sufis employ this word to refer to the formulas of remembrance that a Shaykh orders his students to recite in the morning after the morning (*fajr*) prayer and the evening after the sunset (*magrhib*) prayer."

Wudhu: The act of ritual purification prescribed by the Prophet ohamed, peace be upon him, to precede the act of ritual prayer.

Zawiya: literally "Corner": The gathering place for the *dhikr* of a Sufi order. (Also known in Persian and Turkish as *Tekkiya*, *Khanaqah*, or *Durga*.)

Ziyara: a visit. In the Sufi context *ziyara* is a visit to a sacred place, which could be the grave of one of the saints or to a living saint or gathering of *fuqara*.

BIBLIOGRAPHY

Abdullah, Sayyid Omar, The Concept of Felicity in Medieaval Islamic Philosophy, Thesis, Oriel College, Oxford, UK, 1963.

Abu Sa'id Fazlu'llah bin Abi'l Khair, The Secret of God's Mystical Oneness, translated by John O'Kane, Mazda Publishers, Costa Mesa, CA, 1992.

Ad-Darqawi, Al-'Arabi. Letters of a Sufi Master. Translated by Titus Burckhardt. Fons Vitae, Louisville, KY, 1998.

Addas, Claude, Quest for the Red Sulphur: The Life of Ibn 'Arabi, translated from the French by Peter Kingsley, Islamic Texts Society Golden Palm Series, Cambridge, 1993.
Addas, Claude, The Voyage of No Return, translated from the French by David Streight, Islamic Texts Society, Cambridge, UK, 2000.

Al-'Alawi, Ahmad, Two Who Attained, translated by Leslie Cadavid, Fons Vitae, Louisville, KY, 2005.

Al-Bayhaqi, Imam, The Seventy-Seven Branches of Faith, translated by Abdal Hakim Murad, The Quilliam Press Ltd., Dorton, Bucks., UK, 1990

Al-Ghazali, Abu Hamid Muhammad ibn Muhammad, The Duties of Brotherhood in Islam, translated by Muhtar Holland, The Islamic Foundation, Leicester UK, 1980.
Al-Ghazali, Abu Hamid Muhammad ibn Muhammad, Invocations and Supplications (Kitab al-adhkar wa'l-da'awat), translated by K. Nakamura, Islamic Texts Society, Cambridge UK, 1990
Al-Ghazali, Abu Hamid Muhammad ibn Muhammad, Letter to a Disciple (Ayyuha'l-Walad), translated by Tobias Mayer, Islamic Texts Society, Cambridge, 2005.
Al-Ghazali, Abu Hamid Muhammad ibn Muhammad, Music and

Singing, translated by Duncan Black MacDonald, Islamic Book Trust, Kuala Lumpur, 2009

Al-Ghazali, Abu Hamid Muhammad ibn Muhammad. The Ninety-Nine Beautiful Names of God (*al-Maqsad al-asna fi sharh asma Allah al-husna*), translated by David B. Burrel and Nazih Daher, Islamic Texts Society, Cambridge UK, 1992.

Al-Haddad, Imam 'Abdallah Ibn 'Alawi, Gifts for the Seeker, translated by Mostafa Al-Badawi, Fons Vitae, Louisville, KY, 2003.

Al-Haddad, Imam 'Abdallah Ibn 'Alawi, The Sublime Treasures, translated by Mostafa al-Badawi, Fons Vitae, Louisville, KY, 2008.

Al-Haddad, Habib Ahmad Mashhur, Key to the Garden, translated by Mostafa Al-Badawi, The Quilliam Press, London, 1990.

Al-Hujwiri, Ali bin Uthman. Kashf Al Mahjub. Translated by Reynold A. Nicholson. Taj Company, Delhi, 1982.

Al-Iskandari, Ibn Ata'illah, The Book of Wisdom (*Al-Hikam*). Translated by Victor Danner, Paulist Press, New York, 1978.

Al-Iskandari, Ibn Ata'illah. The Subtle Blessings in the Saintly Lives of Abu Al-Abbas Al-Mursi and His Master Abu Al-Hasan (*Kitab Lata'if al-Minan fi Manaqib Abi'l-Abbas al-Mursi wa Shaykhihi Abi'l-Hasan*). Translated by Nancy Roberts. Fons Vitae, Louisville, Ky, 2005.

Al-Iskandari, Ibn Ata'illah, The Book of Illumination (*Kitab al-Tanwir fi Isqat al-Tadbir*), Translated by Scott Kugle, Fons Vitae, Louisville, KY, 2005.

Al-Iskandari Ibn Ata'illah, The Key to Salvation (*Miftah al-Falah wa Misbah al-Arwah*), translated by Mary Ann Koury Danner, The Islamic Texts Society Golden Palm Series, Cambridge, 1996.

Al-Jawziyya, Ibn Qayyim. The Invocation of God (*Al-Wabil*

al-Sayyib min al-Kalim al-Tayyib), translated by Abdurrahman Fitzgerald and Moulay Youssef Slitine. ITS, Cambridge, 2000.
Al-Jerrahi, Sheikh Muzaffer Ozak, The Unveiling of Love, translated by Muhtar Holland, Inner Traditions, New York, 1981.

Al-Jerrahi, Muzaffer Ozak, The Unveiling of Love. Translated by Muhtar Holland, Inner Traditions International, New York, 1981.

Al-Jilani, Abd al-Qadir, The Secret of Secrets, interpreted by Shaykh Tosun Bayrak al-Jerrahi al-Halveti, Islamic Texts Society, Cambridge UK, 1992.
Al-Jilani, Abdul Qadir. *Futuh Al-Ghaib* (Revelations of the Unseen). Translated by M. Aftab-ud-Din Ahmad. Sh. Muhammad Ashraf, Lahore, 1986.
Ansari, Khwaja Abdullah. Intimate Conversations (*Munajat*), translated by W.M. Thackston, Jr., Paulist Press, New York, 1978.

Al-Qushayri,Abu'l Qasim Abd al-Karim, Principles of Sufism, translated by B.R. von Schlegell, Islamic Book Trust, Kuala Lumpur, 2004.

'Attar, Faridu'd-Din, The Speech of the Birds (*Mantiqu'-Tair*), presented by Peter Avery, Islamic Texts Society, Cambridge, 1998.
'Attar, Farid Al-Din. Muslim Saints and Mystics (*Tadhkirat al-Auliya*). Translated by A.J. Arberry. Arkana, London, 1990.

Chittick, William C. Me & Rumi: The Autobiography of Shamsi Tabriz, Fons Vitae, Louisville, Kentucky, 2004
Chittick, William C. The Sufi Doctrine of Rumi, World Wisdom Inc., Bloomington, Indiana, 2005

Chodkiewicz, Michel, Seal of the Saints, translated from the

French by Liadain Sherrard, Islamic Texts Society, Cambridge, UK 1993

Cornell, Vincent J., Realm of the Saint: Power and Authority in Moroccan Sufism, University of Texas Press, Austin, 1998.

Hafiz-i Shirazi, Khwaja Shams ud-Din Muhammad, The Diwan (The Green Sea of Heaven: Fifty ghazals from the Diwan of Hafiz), translated by Elizabeth T. Gray, Jr. White Cloud Press, Ashland, Oregon, 1995.

Ibn Al 'Arabi, Muhyideen, Divine Sayings: 101 Hadith Qudsi: The *Mishkat al-Anwar* of Ibn 'Arabi, translated by Stephen Hirtenstein and Martin Notcutt, Al Anqa Publishing, Oxford, 2004.

Ibn Ajiba, Ahmad, The Autobiography (*Fahrasa*) of a Moroccan Saint, translated from the Arabic by Jean Louis Michon, translated from the French by David Streight, Fons Vitae, Louisville, Kentucky, 1999.

Ibn Al-Habib, Mohamed, The Noble Litany, translated by Abdul Rahman Fitzgerald.

Ibn Al Sabbagh, The Mystical Teachings of al-Shadhili (*Durrat al-Asrar wa Tuhfat al-Abrar*), translated by Elmer H. Douglas, State University of New York Press, 1993.

'Isa, Shaykh Abd Al-Qadir, Realities of Sufism. Translated by Suraqah Abdul Aziz. Sunni Publications, The Netherlands, 2009.

Lings, Martin, Sufi Poems: A Mediaeval Anthology, Islamic Texts Society, Cambridge, 2004.
Lings, Martin, A Sufi Saint of the Twentieth Century: Shaikh

Ahmad Al-Alawi – His Spiritual Heritage and Legacy, Islamic Text Society Golden Palm Series, Cambridge, 1993.

Lings, Martin, What is Sufism?, University of California Press, Berkley, California, 1977.

Rizvi, Saiyid Athar Abbas, A History of Sufism in India, Volumes One and Two, Munshairam Manoharlal Publishers Pvt. Ltd., New Delhi, 1986.

Shu'ayb, Abu Madyan, The Way of Abu Madyan. Compiled and Translated by Vincent J. Cornell, Islamic Texts Society, Cambridge, 1996.

Suhrawardi, Shaikh Shahabu-u'd-din 'Umar b. Muhammad, *The Awarif-u'l-Ma'arif,* translated by Lieut.-Col. H. Wilberforce Clarke, Sh. Muhammad Ashraf, Lahore, 1973.

PHOTOGRAPHY

Cover - Peter Sanders

Appearances - Shems Friedlander

The Hidden - Peter Sanders

The Caretaker - Shakir Massoud-Priest

A Black Ant on a Black Stone - Peter Sanders

All Night Long - Peter Sanders

The Glance - Peter Sanders

The Unseeen - Peter Sanders

The Illuminated - Unknown (*Courtesy Peter Sanders*)

First Light - John Gulliver (*Courtesy Peter Sanders*)

The Beacon - Peter Sanders

Twenty-Four Hours - Peter Sanders

The Centenarian - Unknown (*Courtesy Peter Sanders*)

Transmission - Unknown

The Cure - Unknown

Majesty - Peter Sanders

River of Heaven (*Courtesy Shaykh Abdul Ghani Saleh Al-Ja'fari*)

Three Hundred - Unknown

The English Saint - Shems Friedlander

Gazing at the House - Unknown

The Beloved - Peter Sanders

Ambassador Extraordinaire... - Peter Sanders

Song and Dance - 2 photos by Shems Friedlander

The Living - Peter Sanders (*Grave of Habib Ahmad Mashhur Al Haddad*)

Direct from Paradise - Unknown (*Courtesy Peter Sanders*)

The author sleeping - Peter Sanders

Full Circle - Peter Sanders

About the Author - Abu'l Qasim Spiker

Calligraphy in the Introduction by Hajj Mahmoud Ibrahim Salama
Calligraphy of the Divine Name in Transfigured Night by Soraya Syed

10020075R00117

Printed in Great Britain
by Amazon.co.uk, Ltd.,
Marston Gate.